Called to Love

Called to Love

*Discernment, Decision
Making and Ministry*

Raymond Tomkinson

scm press

© Raymond Tomkinson 2012

Published in 2012 by SCM Press
Editorial office
13–17 Long Lane,
London, EC1A 9PN, UK

SCM Press is an imprint of Hymns Ancient & Modern Ltd
(a registered charity)
13A Hellesdon Park Road
Norwich NR6 5DR, UK

www.scmpress.co.uk

British Library Cataloguing in Publication data

A catalogue record for this book is available
from the British Library

978-0-334-04417-8
Kindle edition 978-0-334-04467-3

Originated by The Manila Typesetting Company
Printed and bound by
CPI Group (UK) Ltd, Croydon, CR0 4YY

Contents

Dedication

For my wife Rose, daughter Marian,
son-in-law Rod and grandson Jacob

Foreword

Martyn Percy

Strange though this may sound, the two key questions that face every person at any theological college are these: Who do you say that I am? And, by the way, who on earth am I? It would be a rather odd seminarian that did not find himself or herself asking these questions at some or several points during their training and formation. For the essence of training and formation is to undergo something of a transition – to move from our most cherished spiritual securities and favoured faith foundations into new, strange and unfamiliar theological and ecclesial territories. It can be disarming and unsettling. The old routines that got you there – for so long the manna that sustained you on the journey – are suddenly disrupted by new people and ideas and unfamiliar patterns of worship, prayer and study.

Understandably, many object to this. Theological colleges can quickly become places that are characterized – unfairly as it happens – as venues that foster doubt, nourish vagueness, and even corrode faith. Yet this journey – one of movement from security to the uncertainty that accompanies exploration – is precisely where God wants us to be. For Jesus teaches us often and best when we are at our most open.

The Australian theologian and educationalist Denham Grierson says that this process of 'de-tribalization' is 'alarming to some, threatening to most and determining for all…' He likens it, albeit rather strongly, to joining an army: stripped of our former identity, with new codes and rules, even perhaps new uniforms, we are re-educated and disciplined into a new kind of personal and collective responsibility. This, of course, is not to say that a seminary

ix

is a kind of theological boot camp. Yet Grierson makes a good point. In the transitional space of theological training and formation, those embarking on the journey to become clergy often find themselves estranged from their immediate past, and unsure of what the present and future might look like. Yet this is part of God's calling. To be called out of the past and to be formed and re-formed in the present and future.

This is a transitional phase. This is a time for change and renewal. And although the repercussions should be evident for many years to come, and welcome at that, some sort of balance is eventually restored. Seminarians will be able to say who they are. And also who Jesus is. The time at theological college is a time, therefore, of intense journeying. And though it may sometimes seem costly and counter-intuitive, it is usually worth the cost of going with the flow, and persevering.

If I may be allowed a personal reflection on this, there can be something of the 'white knuckle ride' about theological training. Not long ago, I found myself, on the final day of our holiday, with my two teenage boys at a 'Water Theme Park' in Brisbane ('Wet and Wild', I think it was called), who thought I might enjoy this experience. At some point in the afternoon I came under considerable pressure to join them in a large rubber ring, going down a ride called 'The Tornado'. Helpfully, my sons added that if I joined them on the ride, my extra weight would add significant value to the thrill of their experience. Reluctantly, I agreed. I had even more reason to doubt the wisdom of this as we ascended several flights of steps, such that the people below seemed very small indeed. We got to the top, and climbed into a rubber ring. Then we set off.

It was terrifying. Seventy kilos of humanity (in my case) hurtled down small tubes of water at a rate of knots. I quickly discovered that the best way to cope with imminent destruction was to look backwards – where I had come from, and not where I was going. Congratulating myself on the brilliance of this strategy at 70 miles an hour, I was unprepared for the mid-point of the 'ride' – the aptly named 'Vortex' (it does exactly what it says on the tin) – where we seemed to revolve around faster and faster upside down and inside out, in ways that I did not think were humanly possible. Eventually, we landed. The boys screaming with delight. Me, finishing my prayers; and querying the viability of my future life in relation to my heart rate.

My point is that in the hurtling speed of training and formation, there are both thrills and disorientations. But the journey, as much as we make it, also comes to us. And it is therefore vital, in a time and place of transition, for any seminarian to pause and reflect. To try and find some peace and space in training to reflect on who you are; what God has called you to; what you are becoming; and who Jesus was, is and is becoming to you.

As Raymond Tomkinson shows in this fresh, original, remarkable and timely book, the processes of transition in training and formation in ministry set before us a number of questions. The same Jesus who asks you 'who do you say that I am' also asks 'and by the way, who are you?' The question is ever before us, as we commit ourselves to the calling God has laid upon us: to become the person, people and communities that God is forming us into. If we are faithful, God will surely answer us: 'you are my beloved, my chosen one – the one in whom I delight to go and bear fruit – fruit that will last'. Raymond's wise and spiritually astute book, born of rich experience and deep reflection, will repay careful, meditative reading for all in ministry. It beckons us to walk together along that road, and follow the Lord of the journey: he who is the bridge and guide through all our transitions.

Acknowledgements

I am deeply grateful to all whose experiences of transitions in ministry have contributed to this book. Among them are the 'Cuddesdon Twelve' who took part in the research project that inspired it. Thanks are due to members of the Cuddesdon community and to other colleagues in ministry whose advice, experience, encouragement and support have been invaluable in bringing it to publication. Particular thanks to Revd Canon Professor Martyn Percy, Principal of Ripon College Cuddesdon, for writing the Foreword. Thanks are also due to Dr Natalie Watson, Senior Commissioning Editor of SCM Press, for her faith in the project and her encouragement and support throughout.

Some of the reflections in this book are the fruit of several decades of personal experience in a number of ministerial settings so I wish to record my thanks to those who have guided me in ministry. Most of all I want to record my thanks to my dear wife, Rose, for her love and support in all I undertake. During the past 37 years, we have journeyed together, and by the grace of God, have navigated many transitions in our own ministries.

Introduction

A sudden, heavy shower caused Caroline and Graham to dash for shelter in a small octagonal summerhouse in the corner of the retreat house grounds. Arriving simultaneously, from different directions, Graham opened the door to allow Caroline to step in first. The summerhouse contained two garden chairs. Seated, the occupants were knee to knee. It took only seconds for them to decide to abandon their self-imposed silence, the weather being the obvious topic of conversation. They had seen each other across the chapel and in the dining room but they hadn't met. They introduced themselves and exchanged information about where they ministered and sought connections between themselves. Graham explained that he was nearing the end of his annual five day retreat and Caroline explained that she had arrived only the day before and was just settling in.

'What brings you on retreat, Caroline?' asked Graham. Caroline explained that her curacy post would end in a few months' time and that she was beginning to think about what she should do next. Her bishop, her incumbent and her friends in ministry had made various suggestions. She had come away on retreat to give herself space to think through possibilities and to seek God's will for her. Graham reciprocated by relating how he was very happily settled in his post as team rector, a post he had held for nine years; or at least he had been happily settled until the day before when something in one of the readings at Morning Prayer had disturbed his sense of contentment. Now he had begun to wonder if God was calling him to move on in his ministry.

It had stopped raining but neither of them noticed as they continued to discuss how one discerns God's will when considering a move. They shared their experience of making decisions and they reflected on whether or not God has some grand plan for us which we must second guess by trial and error. Was our God like the Olympian gods of ancient Greek mythology toying with us like chess pieces on a board? They agreed that God is not like that and they considered whether or not God has a strong view about where we go or what we do so long as our intention is to love and to serve. Surely, they argued, we are called to love and our serving will flow from that?

How we discern God's will for us and for the Church as a whole, how we make decisions and theological reflection on how we are called to love are the themes explored in this book. The reader is encouraged not only to reflect on their approach to decision making but to consider what theological reflection models they use to reach what I have termed a 'discerned decision' in respect of a transition in ministry. We consider, too, whether we make decisions about a ministerial transition in a markedly different way from how we make other decisions.

Secular academic learning on the theory of decision making is called upon to aid our exploration. We consider the value and the God-givenness of such learning and how it relates to the practices of the Church. John Swinton and Harriet Mowat, much respected practical theologians (2006, p. 8), state that:

> The practices of the Church cannot be understood as ontologically separate or different from the practices of the world. Both occur within God's creation and both are caught up in God's redemptive movement towards the world. Within a creation which is profoundly fallen and broken, all human beings, including the Church, fall short of the good purposes of God. In that respect all human practices are inadequate, including the practices of the Church. There is, therefore, significant similarity and continuity between the practices of the Church and the practices of the world.

The themes addressed in this book are illustrated by stories and anecdotes, some metaphoric, some parabolic, and all included to encourage the reader to make connections between the theories expounded and their own experience in Christian ministry. This book is a gathering of experience of how God works in and through the Church's ministry. It has not been my purpose to offer a comprehensive description of transition in every expression of ministry. As St Paul reminds us (1 Cor. 12—14) there are a variety of gifts and ministries among God's people and no two ministries will be identical. Illustrations are drawn from the experience of those embarking on ordained ministry and from those with experience of transition at different stages in ministerial life.

Material came, too, from my own observations and experience of listening to ordinands and clergy over many years. It offers a panoramic and contextual view of aspirations, hopes and expectations, and adds a barometric appraisal to the other gathered data, some of which was gleaned from semi-structured interviews. I have reflected on how, as a researcher, an observer and as a story-hearer as well as a storyteller, I may have affected the material presented to the reader. I concluded that my experience would provide valid and useful additional data, but I accepted that I would not be dispassionate; I am part of the experience, and I have a standpoint epistemology and an authorial eye. Denscombe (2007, p. 80) advocates that the researcher adopt the role of a 'stranger' and advises that the researcher faithfully include all aspects of the interviewee's account including 'those comments that appear contradictory, irrational or even bizarre'. If I was to think of myself as a 'stranger' it was important to try to 'behold' the phenomenon and to ask questions that a stranger might ask, and to consider what is it like for ministers in transition: what is the *zeitgeist*?

The stories I employ to promote resonance and reflection fall broadly into three categories. Some stories are fictional but the issues at the heart of those stories are based in fact. Some stories are true accounts and only work with integrity if not fictionalized. Here, I have sought and gained the originator's permission and have merely changed names and places to protect their privacy.

For the most part, stories have been referenced in the text with a bold heading so that they can be picked out more easily if they are to be used to encourage group discussion.

Running like a spine through this book are accounts of the experience of twelve women and men who shared their experience of moving on from Ripon College Cuddesdon (RCC), an Anglican seminary near Oxford, to serve as curates in parishes across England. Their experience makes a contribution to an ongoing discourse about how to reduce the incidence of curacy breakdown. The twelve participants comprised six ordinands exploring curacy options and six curates who had, in recent years, experienced the process of securing a curacy. I refer to them as the 'Cuddesdon Twelve'. They have generously given permission for their responses, made in a questionnaire and in interviews, to be used in this book.

As a former Visiting Spiritual Director and, more recently, Chaplain of RCC, I have had the enormous privilege of being in a community of ordinands yielding, each year, around 60 women and men for ordination. I hear many accounts of how ordinands approach the decision about a curacy. It is not my job to advise them which curacy offer to accept but to accompany them as they explore God's will for them. I do, however, help them to frame the questions they need to ask of themselves and of others. Ordinands may be wrestling with the, sometimes, conflicting demands and desires of other stakeholders in the process: spouse, family, diocesan officers, to whom they have to account for their decisions. Some ordinands struggle to explain their dilemma and, when they reach a discerned decision, may struggle to articulate their reasons for reaching it. RCC prides itself on the diversity of traditions within the Anglican spectrum that are represented within the college community. This makes for a richness of Christian ecclesial tradition and so enriches the well from which my illustrations are drawn. The twelve women and men whose experience has contributed to this book come from different traditions within the Church and vary in age from 29 to 56. It was important that they knew and understood with whom their contributions might be shared. Respondents were reassured that every effort would be made to protect their identity but without a guarantee that a discerning reader wouldn't identify them and so they were given every opportunity to withdraw their contribution (Bell 2005, et al.). Binding up their gathered offerings and their wide-ranging contributory accounts has been like spinning threads of ecclesial and secular academic learning to produce a strong cord of evidence employed in this book to help our reflection. This academic drawstring is subsidiary to the reflection but offers cognitive frameworks for that reflection. Recurring like an anthemic refrain in this book, the Cuddesdon Twelve are the chief storytellers.

This is not to say that the book might be useful only to ordinands or the recently ordained. Themes explored and discussed are illustrated from a range of ministerial experiences, settings, and transitions ranging from the beginning of ordained ministry to retirement and beyond. The issues raised in reflection on the experience of those beginning their ordained ministerial journey have resonance with issues occurring at other stages of ordained ministerial life. Such reflection may be an anamnesis of the reader's own early experience and may rekindle, for some, the flame of zeal we first felt.

This book is a phenomenological study. The aim has been to consider the world view of the storytellers. I hope to promote response and reaction to their accounts: recognizing that the world view of other stakeholders in the storytellers' ministerial transitions may have a perspective which challenges the views expressed here. I hope that may be so. Although I have used story to illustrate certain themes I have not always drawn conclusions from them but have left the reader to draw their own! Denscombe (2007, p. 78) suggests that phenomenological research is 'seeing things through the eyes of others' and that the phenomenologist's task is to 'present matters as closely as possible to the way that those concerned understand them'. Swinton and Mowat (2006, p. 106) argue that the aim of phenomenology is to determine what an experience means to a person quite apart from any theoretical overlay that might be put on it by the researcher, and to provide a comprehensive and rich description of it.

It has been said that qualitative designs in research have no real value, but it has been argued (Robson 2002, p. 5) that a qualitative research design is not unscientific if it is carried out in a systematic and principled fashion. Hammersley (2000, pp. 393–405) provides a well-argued defence of qualitative designs against attacks on their relevance to policy-making and practice. Robson (2002) argues for the value of qualitative design for people-oriented organizations because the work can evolve, unfold and develop during the research, yielding (arguably) a richer conclusion. This research lent itself well to a qualitative approach since a quantitative approach would be unlikely to get to the heart of what Swinton and Mowat term 'the thing itself'. Commenting on phenomenology, they state that it is:

a philosophy of experience that attempts to understand the ways in which meaning is constructed in and through human experience. This perspective views a person's lived experience (the thing itself) of and within the world as the foundation of meaning. It seeks to set aside any assumptions about the object of the inquiry, and build up a thorough and comprehensive description of the thing itself'. (2006, p. 106)

Gillham (2000, p. 10) suggests that 'qualitative methodologies focus primarily on the kind of evidence (what people tell you they do) that will enable you to understand the meaning of what is going on'. Gillham continues: 'Their great strength is that they illumine issues and turn up possible explanations: essentially a search for meaning – as is all research.'

This study has had an interpretivist lean. It could be argued that there is no place in a phenomenological study for this because the storytellers world view cannot be my view; however, there is an epistemology of what is observed by me as well as an epistemology distilled from the data gathered from others. In claiming an interpretivist steer I am also owning the likelihood that my own experience and relationship with the participants and storytellers is bound to influence how I hear or receive the data but arguing that my own role as a participant observer will thicken the description. It is interpretivist, too, because I have chosen from the data gathered themes to help guide the reader to consider how they decide to move on in ministry.

I

'Why restless . . .?'

How are we to understand human restlessness? As something to be worked against? As a gift from God or as a characteristic of God? The traditional hymn 'As pants the hart for cooling streams' includes the line: 'Why restless, why cast down, my soul?' The words of the hymn are based on Psalm 42 which, together with Psalm 43, are a song of lament by God's faithful people who long for return to their homeland. The sentence which inspired the hymn line forms part of a refrain. In their version of the biblical text, written in 1696, hymn-writers Nahum Tate and Nicholas Brady chose to use the word 'restless' to describe the spiritual 'place' the people of God found themselves to be in. Some translations of the Hebrew biblical text offer a more turbulent interpretation: a profound sense of lamentation and grief, an expression of deep heartache. If it is 'restlessness' then it is the anxiety-based, pacing-of-the-floor sort of restlessness.

The version authorized for use in churches throughout the land (the King James Version) and in use when Tate and Brady wrote this hymn has: 'Why are you cast down, O my soul, and why are you disquieted within me?', but they chose to go with the word 'restlessness' rather than 'disquieted'. Tate and Brady, in their choice of word, touch upon something of our own experience and on that of Christian thinkers and spiritual writers through the ages. For the purpose of this reflection, therefore, we might stay with 'restless' and explore it as a 'given' in human experience before we go on to consider 'disquiet' and 'cast down' as motivators for transitions in Christian ministry.

Restlessness is not only a feature of human experience: it can be a good thing! Restlessness is a symptom of energy; of the dynamic of human life. It is partly what gets us out of bed in the morning! Echoing something of the experience of longing felt by God's ancient people and expressed in Psalms 42 and 43, at some level, we also experience a restless longing that energizes us to seek and to find the living God: a God so far out of our reach that we cannot know him and yet so deep inside us that we cannot but find him. It is an unrelenting and restless inward and outward journey as we scan the earth and the depths of our being for his presence.

The Canadian priest Richard Rolheiser (1998, p. 3) describes the tension between intimacy and distance with God (this side of heaven) as an 'aching' or a 'restlessness'. This dynamic of restlessness is described, famously, by Augustine of Hippo (354–430), who prays: 'You have made us for yourself, Lord, and our hearts are restless until they rest in you' (Blaiklock on Augustine, 1983). The energy of aching or restlessness is part and parcel of the dynamic of the God–humankind relationship and symptomatic of a healthy spirituality. It is the constant ignition spark that fires our transitions and can be experienced as a drawing towards love, creativity, adventure and a future beyond our limited present.

Rolheiser (1998) describes spirituality as 'what we do with our unrest' and as being 'about what we do with the fire inside us; about how we channel our eros'. He suggests there is 'a fundamental dis-ease, an unquenchable fire that renders us incapable, in this life, of ever coming to full peace'.

In an earlier work (1979, p. 65), Rolheiser describes how 'all of us experience within ourselves a certain restlessness and insatiability'. He suggests that 'our hearts and minds are so fashioned that they are never satisfied, always restless'. He goes on to describe how religious thinkers have called this phenomenon by different names, such as 'the spark of the divine in us' and that philosophers have referred to it as 'the desire of the part to return to the whole', stating that the Greeks had two names for it: '*nostos*', a certain homesickness within the human heart and '*eros*', a relentless erotic pull towards whatever we perceive as good. I am deeply grateful to Father Rolheiser for this succinct description.

Seeking stillness

I suggest that, in association with this intrinsic restlessness, deep inside all of us there is a longing for stillness. It is a longing for the stillness of arrival in the vast heart of the Father's love: a place where we can rest contented. This longing is difficult to articulate. We come close to it in what I regard as the shortest and yet one of the deepest prayers we can pray. It is the word 'O'. Pray it many ways and see if it does not say so much about longing! There is a deep sigh in most of us if we take the trouble to listen for it. 'O' is the great word of Advent. If we used no other in our prayers we would have prayed so much. The Great 'Os', the great Advent Antiphons, are a gift to us from our Christian heritage. Each antiphon begins with an 'O'. It is an 'O' of aspiration and longing. It is the 'O' of us all who, as stewards of the mysteries of God, carry its preciousness into a world filled with unidentified godly longing. The hymn 'O come! O Come! Emmanuel' is based on those ancient antiphons and we might do worse than to stay with that one phrase as a mantra, gradually allowing it to be distilled down into a single 'O' or even a sigh from deep within us. It will be a sigh of longing and yearning. Notice how the exercise stills us yet energizes us to seek God!

Our experience is that although we know or glimpse God's love, stillness eludes us for most of the time. Many people in Christian ministry are frantically busy and, when we have time to reflect, we ponder on why it is that we have no time to reflect! We wonder if our inability to be still is some fault in us; a fault that must be overcome if we are to grow spiritually. We work on being still. At first it is a self-conscious competence but, with practice, stillness can seep into our being from the exterior discipline of trying not to move. Eventually, we can be busy about many things yet know a centre of stillness in which we can dwell and in which we can meet God. The tiniest centre of stillness can become for us a vast cavern of inner stillness. For most of us, Christian ministry brings a range of activity as we rush from one pastoral or liturgical task to another. The busier we are the more we need to find stillness. A retreat or 'time out' in a place which engenders stillness helps but the cultivation of a still centre will, paradoxically, energize us as we go about God's business.

We look to the past to consider how iconic figures in our history approached the subject of restlessness, but we argue that they may not have had the pressures we have. We look to the ministry of Jesus and note how busy he was and yet how he managed to find time to relax with friends at Bethany, or to commune with his Father on a mountainside. We may admire the balance of contemplation and activity that is modelled for us and we may aspire to something of it.

The rhythm of activity and stillness is something we acquire either through discipline and practice or through a natural inclination. It is not dissimilar to the rhythm of sleep and wakefulness that our body instinctively regulates. The rhythm of our heart models rest and contraction: a pulsation that keeps us alive. We know that when that pulsation is erratic or irregular, speeds up too much or slows down too much, then we have a problem that needs addressing. Balance needs to be restored. So it is with our lifestyle balance, our work–rest balance; but it is not my purpose, in this book, to address how to achieve that balance, but rather to encourage the reader to look beneath the frameworks of practice to the fundamentals of restlessness. Here we consider restlessness as the energizer of transitions in ministry and look to the source of that restlessness, to the potential God-givenness of our restlessness, and consider it as a reflection of God's own rhythmic pattern of stillness and activity. We consider the pulsating dynamic of a God who energizes us: who is God the quickener of our soul. The story of two travellers may help us in our reflection on stillness and restlessness.

Janet and Geoff's story

Janet and Geoff decided to take a 'turn' around the deck. They had just eaten a delicious lunch. The sea air was refreshing though the visibility was poor. All they could see was the sea! According to the deck steward they were not far from land but they could not see the coast. It mattered little. They were away! They were afloat with no clear view in any direction. They were enjoying the cruise they had promised themselves for many years. It seemed incredible that they had been in Christian ministry for just over 40 years. At last, they had retired. As they walked they talked of many things, some of them inconsequential; the cruise ship, the other passengers, the food. Between snatches of conversation one or other of them sighed. Finally, and after a period of silence, Janet said: 'Ah well.' 'What does that mean?' asked her husband. Janet thought for a few moments before responding. She thought of the wonderful 'send-off' the parishes had given her: the gifts, the bicycle, the luggage for the cruise, the vouchers for a 'city break' later in the year. She realized, from the choice of gifts, that her parishioners thought of her as a person who was never still: someone who loved a new adventure: someone mobile. Janet thought of the last conversation she had had with her spiritual director. She had asked Janet what, in her retirement, she looked forward to most. Without hesitation Janet had replied that she looked forward to being still. Janet admired stillness in those she had met or to whom she had ministered. She had read about being still and remembered being quite moved by Michael Ramsey's book *Be Still and Know*. Whenever Psalm 46 came up in Morning or Evening Prayer, she would read the verse from which Ramsey (1982, p. 6) had taken the title of his book, and she would sigh.

Remembering that Geoff had asked her a question Janet responded with another: 'Geoff, am I a hopelessly restless person?' Geoff laughed. He said: 'You might be restless, Janet, but I don't think you are discontent.' Janet shared her musings with Geoff, and they laughed about the irony of their circumstance. They were on a cruise to celebrate their retirement. They were walking briskly around the deck of a ship careering through the North Sea celebrating the opportunity to be still!

Geoff makes an important distinction. Restlessness and discontent are not the same thing. Janet longs for stillness, but are we ever truly still? There are many excellent books on how to find stillness or exercises in becoming still (how about that for a contradiction in terms!). As we try to sit very still for a few moments and try to follow all the advice for centring ourselves we begin to notice our breathing. Our lungs continue their pattern of expansion and contraction. We breathe in. We breathe out. Generally we are less conscious of the blood coursing through our arteries and veins busy delivering fresh supplies of oxygen to peripheral tissues and busy taking away impurities for other transport systems of our body to deal with. Our ears are ever alert to the sounds around us, bringing challenges of concentration. A lot of the time, being still is hard work! But are we ever truly still? Even after death there is a settling of organs and tissue. Even post mortem our minds might be at rest but our bodies continue to settle and to fragment: 'earth to earth; dust to dust'. Transition continues. Moving from life to death and to life beyond death is a transition in itself: a subject we return to, briefly, at the end of this book.

Contentedness

Janet and Geoff are, for the most part, content. They can look back on a full life; children, grandchildren, friends and many years of ministry. If they are discontent it is with some aspects of the way the world is; injustice, oppression, poverty. They still want to make a difference to the quality of other people's lives. They still find energy for causes close to their hearts, but they would say, of themselves, that they are content. They have learned to appreciate what they can and what they cannot do. A familiar prayer, attributed to Teresa of Avila, is written and framed on a wall in their home: 'Grant me, O Lord, the serenity to accept the things I cannot change; the courage to change the things I can; and the wisdom to know the difference.'

Of course, Janet has not retired from ministry. She has merely retired from a full-time post. Like so many retired clergy Janet will find herself busier than ever! Making the transition into retirement ministry is explored further in Chapter 6. Here, we consider how restlessness initiates or energizes transition.

Restless love

Life is dynamic. It is full of movement; graceful, clumsy, voluntary or involuntary movement. If we are made in the image and likeness of God (as the writer of the book of Genesis testifies), then perhaps our dynamic restlessness is not only a gift from God but is a feature of God's self. We hold that God is love (1 John 4.16b), and love, to be love, has to be dynamic: an oscillation between the lover and the beloved. We will explore the dynamic of love again in Chapter 7.

Restlessness, we may then conclude, is not a twenty-first-century dis-ease. It is a feature of created life. It is a feature of Christian life and ministry, because we are bound up in the restless love of God for us and our corresponding and reciprocal restless love for God and our neighbour. Was there ever a time when this was not so? Since God is love and is from eternity, the answer must be 'no'. Consider the account of the beginning of all things (Gen.1.1–3). The writer attempts to describe life before life, but cannot do so without some sense of movement.

The presence of God at the genesis of creation is described obscurely; the key words translate from the Hebrew as a rushing wind: 'a wind from God swept over the face of the waters' (Gen.1.2). Another version of the same text (Revised English Bible) describes how the Spirit of God 'hovered' over the surface of the water. The image is one of a large bird. Wenham (2003) supports this, linking it to Deuteronomy 32 where God is symbolized as an eagle hovering over its young to feed them. When we see a bird hover, it is not still. Look closely and we see tiny and frequent wing movements sustaining the bird in mid-air as it adjusts to any prevailing wind. Did the writer of Genesis imagine that the water over which the Spirit of God hovered was without movement: no ripple, no wave? We are offered the image of the earth being 'a formless void' with darkness covering the 'face of the deep'. The presence of God disturbs the form and the deep. The dynamic hovering of God quickens what is still.

As the story of creation unfolds the writer describes change and transition in the creatures which populate the earth. He describes the dynamic of work and Sabbath rest that God models (2.2). Further on the writer describes the transitions that take place in the Garden of Eden as disobedience brings its consequences for Adam and Eve: consequences that bring about a drastic change in lifestyle and location (3.14–end). Love, obedience, choice and transition have always been significant in the life of God's people.

Restlessness, body and spirit; God and neighbour

We are restless for intimacy with God but not to the exclusion of restlessness to share with others the experience of God's love, mercy and grace and to find expression for that love in loving service. It is this 'spirit in man' (Job 32.8) which is the dynamic of the soul; energy that comes from life lived within the dynamic of the Holy Trinity. It is not only the wellspring of prayer but the creature's Spirit-filled, heartfelt response to the Creator through the Son. Sometimes this is experienced in a positive way – as a 'pull' towards love, beauty, creativity and a future beyond our limited present. Desire can show itself as aching pain or delicious hope. Rolheiser (1998) points out that spirituality is what we do with that desire. He suggests that what we do with our longings, both in terms of handling the pain and the hope they bring us, *is* our spirituality.

Restlessness as unsettledness: Anne's story

Anne told her doctor that she didn't think she was in a good place. She had just moved to one of the loveliest towns in the South of England, and her doctor was puzzled and a little offended. Anne explained that her dis-ease was nothing to do with geographical location, but that it was a sense of what Rolheiser (1998) would call becoming 'unglued' and which she correlated to living in chaos. Anne explained that moving house, job, culture, and even a change of water(!) had taken some getting used to. She had not yet established a routine and a sense of order in her life. She didn't want to get 'stuck in a rut', but she was seeking some pattern, some framework, on which to hang her (new) life. In that unsettled state she accused herself of having become rather self-centred and introspective to the exclusion of both God and the world around her. Until she found new friends, a community in which she could feel comfortable and a church where she could find fellowship, she was feeling isolated and in a state of spiritual dis-ease. Anne wasn't asking her doctor to do anything about those things. She was sure the sense of spiritual dis-ease would be resolved. She simply offered a rationale for her current state of ennui which was manifesting itself in a range of physically debilitating symptoms. For Anne, not being in a 'good place' said it all. When we come to consider 'place' we should not rule out geographical location. It has its part to play in a wider understanding of the word.

Christ: the 'place' to be

Many of the spiritual 'greats', such as John of the Cross and Teresa of Avila, have attested to the 'place' of Christ as the place of incarnation. The first place to seek to be is 'in Christ' who is 'in God': to be at one with God, through Christ. It is in that place that they met their Lord and it is the same place where we, too, have our lovers tryst with the Beloved. But Christ's place is the place of the world in which we live: the world he came to redeem. It is the place of the displaced: where he seeks us out and finds us. Therefore, an authentic spirituality will not be divorced from the world and its needs and concerns. Christ is the 'touching place'. Christ is the place to put our restlessness as we search for him in the least likely places. He is the place from which we behold our view of the world. From there we see the plight of our neighbour and so it is from there that we reach out, journey out, our Christ-centred restlessness triggering our ministerial transitions.

Each of us must find our place in Christ and in the world. Both Christ and the world will shape who we are and how we behave. To be in the 'right place' is to be at one with God and our neighbour and to be able to hold, in tension or in balance, the relationship between the two and to live within the dynamic of God, knowing what it means to be a child of God and to be a human being growing into God. We do well to remember the epigram of Athanasius: 'God became human so that human beings might become God.'

Ministerial transitions are expressions of Christ-centred restlessness intrinsically caught up in God's restlessness. Transitions are characterized by a pulsation of activity and rest. It is the 'heartbeat' of a healthy relationship with God. Restlessness is the ignition of the torch which lights our transitions. It is the light of the Holy Spirit.

'Why cast down my soul?'

Earlier we explored the first half of the question in the refrain from Psalms 42 and 43 as transposed by the hymn writers Tate and Brady. Now we consider the second half: 'Why cast down my soul?' adding, from the biblical translation: 'Why are you disquieted within me?' We hear, immediately, the difference between life-giving and energizing restlessness: the longing and yearning for our heavenly homeland that is both generic and organic of humankind and the implicit casualty of being 'cast down'. It is the difference between the way we are and what happens to us, what disquiets us, disturbs us or casts us down. We may ask who or what disturbs us; who or what casts us down. This is not to say that disturbances or life experiences that cast us down do not have the potential to be life-giving. Quite the reverse! Stories abound of how people have found God, have come to faith in Christ and have discovered a fruitful and life-giving pathway of loving service given to God in gratitude for their rescue and recovery. Many will testify to how God rescued them from the mire and how they were sent on their way rejoicing to love and serve the Lord.

We consider what it is that troubles the waters of life and how transitions in ministry can come from times of disquiet within and experiences of being cast down. We reflect on how being disturbed energizes us. We might consider this under three headings: the Holy Spirit as disturber: life crisis as disrupter and bringer of change: and self-generated dis-ease. To some extent these aspects are interconnected. The Holy Spirit has a role and presence in all three aspects.

Transitions in ministry are grounded in continual reference to the will of God. We may not be conscious that this is what we are doing, but if it is not what we are doing we may well lose our way. The conversations we have with God, from the moment we first acknowledge that we may be considering a move, until we have either moved and settled down again or we have become reconciled to staying where we are, contain a tacit question regarding God's will for us. We want and need some affirmation that we are doing the right thing. Consideration of our circumstance, appraisal of our gifts, discussions and negotiations with all parties involved, take place in the presence of God. We, and all the other stakeholders in the transitional process, seek God's goodwill for the venture in prospect.

Our transitional journey is rarely straightforward. There are twists and turns and holes in which to fall. There will be spiritual 'highway robbers' who take from us the reassurances, the affirmations and the satisfiers which encourage us to go on. Such robbers take those precious gems and leave us with mere shiny trinkets of ego, self-serving and narcissism. The result is that we lose our way, at least temporarily. The voice of longing to journey on, which is deep inside us, can be drowned out by the noise and clamour of life events and crises as well as by the purveyors of comforters and satisfiers whose goods claim to bring peace. Sometimes we succumb willingly and sometimes we have been taken to the top of fine 'buildings', spiritual edifices of our own making, and been impressed with the view. Perhaps we have done more than take in the view. Perhaps we have participated in all that has delighted the eye. Then, like the prodigal son (Luke 15.11–end), we have squandered our inheritance and been brought low. Our experience testifies to waywardness and wilfulness. We testify also to the small voice of God and the gentle hand on our elbow that brought us back to the path that leads us to our true home, but not before we have been brought low, cast down and disquieted. Consider Jim's story:

Jim's story

Jim felt disturbed by the Holy Spirit whenever he attended Sunday worship. He sensed he was being called to serve God in ordained

CALLED TO LOVE

ministry, but he couldn't bring himself to give up his occupation
as a stockbroker. He considered self-supporting ministry, but his
dis-ease was not soothed by that prospect. It would have to be full-
time stipendiary ministry. However, Jim could not bring himself to
give up the lifestyle that his considerable income made possible.

A turn in the world financial markets caused his firm to 'crash'.
His own share portfolio became worthless, and the firm could no
longer afford to employ him. He had nothing. His dis-ease continued as he ranted at God and the world because of his misfortune.
His marriage broke up under the pressure of the circumstances.
He was alone and impoverished. He turned his back on God and
the Church, yet every time he walked past a church he felt a dis-
ease that was not about his anger or resentment. He tells the story
of how he was passing a church one Christmas Eve on the way
back from a pub. He joined the congregation for the Midnight
Eucharist more out of sentiment than recovered faith; but it was
the beginning of a slow return to a practising faith and finally to
full-time stipendiary ordained ministry.

God had not given up on Jim even though Jim had practically
given up on himself. Resurrection had come out of a series of
little deaths. God had met him in the darkest places of both his
life circumstances and his inner dis-ease. Jim's painful transition
had brought him to the only fulfilling response: an unconditional
response to the unconditional love of God that beckoned him.
How far this is from any sense that God had cast Jim down into
the abyss! Jim had made choices. He had chosen to fend off the
sense of wholehearted call into ordained ministry. He was rather
like the rich ruler (Luke 18.18–25). He rejected the call to evangelical poverty. He 'became sad; for he was very rich'. He had
chosen to take care of his riches, but the choices he had made
led to the loss of everything. He had also been subject, as many
people in our world today are, to the financial choices made by
others. Ultimately, Jim knew he could not blame such choices on
God. There will be some who will preach that God brought down
the great financial institutions of the world to teach us all a lesson,
but this is a theological perspective I cannot hold. It seems to me
that humanity is capable of doing such a thing all by itself!

In Jim's story we hear of the role of the Holy Spirit as disturber tugging away gently at Jim's elbow, trying to attract him towards heavenly treasure ready to be poured out in the market places where people gather. The same Spirit was quietly sustaining both him and the church that welcomed him that Christmas Eve. The Spirit of reconciliation drew him, touched the hearts of those who heard his story and inspired those who would journey with him in the rediscovery of his vocation. The same Spirit has been with him as he ventured on through subsequent ministerial transitions.

We hear of the role of life circumstances and the consequences of Jim's choices and those of others, of their power to significantly alter the life and fortunes of people they will never meet. Finally we hear of Jim's dis-ease as it resurfaced, as anger and resentment subsided. We hear, too, how sentiment was the igniter of the flame of loving response that would result in devotion and service in the world.

Why restless, why cast down my soul?

In his Foreword to 'Markings', the English poet W. H. Auden quotes Dag Hammarskjøld as stating: 'In our age the road to holiness necessarily passes through the world of action.' The restlessness we explored earlier in this chapter can be channelled into activity of all kinds. Restlessness is like adrenalin; it keeps us prepared to fight or to flee. At the same time, busyness, one of the children of restlessness, can be a mask or a way of ensuring we cannot hear the God who calls us to account for our disquiet. Life events, circumstances and tragedies all shape our lives. People relay stories of how bereavement, divorce, or redundancy were devastating experiences. They tell of how life-threatening illness or the onset of a chronic health condition or an impossible work or home situation caused them to 'take stock': to consider what now is important. God's Spirit can be found at work in adversity, bringing healing and renewal, pathways of hope and fulfilment. We may tell how we found, through friends, family members or strangers, energy to build a new life, to move in a new direction.

A vocation to be married turned into a vocation to embrace the single life. The loss of a job led to training in new skills. The closure of every door except the one marked 'ordination' led to a fulfilling ministry in the service of the gospel.

There may be little or nothing to account for the disquiet we feel. Perhaps we know only that we do not want life to be the same as it is. Perhaps there is no excitement, no sense of adventure. Perhaps we are bored. We do not know what we want: we just know that we want life to be different. Through the disturbance of explicit or implicit disquiet, through being 'cast down' by life circumstances may come new insights into ourselves, into other people, or into the world in general.

For most of us, life-changing transitions do not happen overnight. For many there will have been months or years of being 'cast down', an experience of crippling depression or ennui. There may have been a long period of time with no vision of the way ahead. Rather, we are like Janet and Geoff on that cruise-boat walk: in troubled waters with poor visibility. Transition, at such times, is not up or forward but down or backwards, and possibly a complete disorientation leaving us giddy and confused.

In the next chapter we consider further the role of the Holy Spirit as inspirer and disturber.

2

The End of Contentedness

Come Holy Ghost our souls inspire
and lighten with celestial fire;
thou the anointing Spirit art,
who dost thy sevenfold gifts impart.

The opening verse of this ancient hymn may remind us of a solemn moment during an ordination service. In some traditions the candidate for ordination lies prostrate on the ground: a sign of dying to oneself and complete abandonment to the will of God. That moment in the ordination service is a pledge of lifelong acquiescence to the will of God and an acknowledgement that the living out of that pledge, day after day, year after year, requires the grace of God the Holy Spirit through whose gifting we minister. In this chapter we consider how the Holy Spirit enlivens us, inspires us and disturbs us. We consider ways in which we are moved. To suggest that we are 'moved' implies that there are times when we are still. We explored this a little in the previous chapter, but here we consider that being still might be more about contentedness or even complacency.

The first sign of a God-inspired transition may be the end of contentedness and the beginning of discontent. This is a transition in itself and brings its own challenges. Feelings of guilt mingle with feelings of discomfort and help to frame the question: 'Why am I not content?' Barbara and Judy's story may help us to explore this further.

Barbara and Judy's story

Barbara and her daughter Judy stood back to admire their handiwork. The freshly redecorated spare bedroom was bathed in

afternoon sunlight making the soft tones of the walls and soft fur-
nishings glow. The room would be a warm, calm and welcoming
place for guests. When Barbara and Judy moved into the rectory,
a little more than seven years previously the house had been redecorated throughout. All the walls had been painted in a neutral
'magnolia' colour and all the woodwork had been painted white.
The house had little character but was practical and adequate for
the needs of the occupants. It had taken seven years for Barbara
and Judy to rid the house of magnolia paint! The spare bedroom
was the last room to receive a personality that reflected their own.
As finishing touches were made to the room they felt a deep sense
of satisfaction.

Barbara had accepted the post of rector in this rural multi-parish
benefice with some trepidation. It was a post of 'first responsibility' following a three-year curacy some 30 miles away. She had
wondered if she would cope with rural ministry and with the challenges of six small parishes, each with their own church councils.
The biggest challenge had been to integrate what had been two
benefices into one. For many parishioners Barbara was the first
woman priest they had met and, although the vast majority of
her parishioners welcomed her ministry, there were some among
them who wondered if she would be 'up to the job'. Barbara had
proved to be more than 'up to the job'. She had transformed the
life of the Church in those parts. After seven years the annual
round of parochial events ran like clockwork. Contrary to the expectations of some, congregations had not dwindled. Indeed, they
had slowly grown, a sprinkling of young families here and there
throwing into sharp contrast the core of more elderly parishioners
who had sustained the small church communities in recent years.
She was known universally as 'Our Barbara'.

The move to the benefice house, seven years earlier, had been
timed perfectly: Judy had just finished at primary school. She had
made friends at her local secondary school and now, on a gap
year with university in prospect, Judy looked forward to being
able to catch up with old friends during university vacations.

It was with a contented sigh that Barbara and Judy changed out
of their painting clothes. They toyed with the idea of throwing out

the paint-stained clothes. 'No more painting!' cried Barbara from her bedroom. 'Hurray!' responded Judy from hers.

It was time to put the kettle on. As Barbara passed through the hall on her way to the kitchen, she picked up the church newspaper that had dropped through the letter box. As she waited for the kettle to boil, she sat at the kitchen table absently flicking through the pages, pausing occasionally if something caught her eye. Judy joined her in the kitchen and made the tea. Barbara hadn't noticed that Judy had gone very quiet. 'You OK Jude?' she enquired without looking up. There was no reply. This caught Barbara's attention. She looked up to find Judy standing, arms folded, leaning against the worktop with silent tears running down her cheeks.

'What's the matter, Jude?' she asked as she got up to enfold Judy in a warm embrace. 'Are you thinking of moving on, Mum?' Judy asked very quietly.

'Of course not. Whatever gave you that idea?'

'When I came in, you were looking at the Situations Vacant pages.'

Barbara hadn't noticed that she was doing so and reasoned that even if she had been it didn't mean she was looking for another job. Sometimes, she explained to Judy, it's just nice to see what's going on. Judy was mollified, but Barbara became pensive. She was concerned at how easily upset Judy had been at the possibility that they might move away. She recognized how important the stability of their home had been over Judy's teenage years and how much Judy valued a familiar base to which she would return from her travels and from university, but she hadn't realized how close to the surface were Judy's concerns.

Barbara's thoughts that night were about Judy but also about herself. Had she been looking at the Situations Vacant and if so, why would she? She was very happy where she was; she was now reaping the rewards of her hard work over the seven years. God had blessed her in her obedience to minister in that place and had rewarded her with a contentment beyond her dreams and beyond her experience of life to date. She thanked God for all that she now had; but even as she did so, she ended the prayer quickly in case God came back with: 'That's great, Barbara, but I have something else I want you to do for me.'

She went back down to the kitchen where the newspaper still lay open where she had left it. She scanned the page to reassure herself that she had not been attracted to anything on it. But she had. There it was. A school was looking for a chaplain. Barbara closed the newspaper quickly and, dismissing all thoughts of the matter, went to bed.

One of the most fulfilling aspects of her current ministry had been the opportunity to minister in a small private school. The trustees had quickly welcomed her involvement there and had even paid for her to attend courses to help develop her skills and understanding of the needs of the pupils and of the staff. She had enjoyed teaching a little religious education as well as leading worship. Now that things were running smoothly in the benefice, Barbara had taken to spending up to one day each week at the school. Was God now calling her to take up a full-time post in a school somewhere? Would he do that to her just as she had been feeling so content where she was?

It would be three years before Barbara was appointed chaplain to a school in another part of the country. The idea, which had sprung seemingly from nowhere, had in fact been nurtured in her for many years. Judy's sharp observation and question had caused Barbara to consider her deepest desires and aspirations and to articulate her vision for schools ministry. This articulation did not come out of a time of discontent, but at a time of contentment with what she had been given to do. The idea had been right, but the timing had been wrong. By the time Barbara had taken up her new post, Judy had settled into university and had begun a new personal relationship. Judy was happy for her mum to move on.

There are times when a decision is made in the heart, but it dare not find articulation because it affects other people. We have prayed about it and sensed not so much a command as an invitation. Perhaps it is not even that, but more that we don't think God would disapprove of the plan forming in our mind. The Lord invites us to follow him but he knows our frailty and accepts what we offer. It is possible for us to continue for some time in a way of life or ministry with internal struggles. Inside we might say, 'I cannot go on with this.' We are not always conscious that those who care about us have become aware of our struggle and long for us to declare it. They long to tell us that they understand and they want to help us through it. We may not want to express what we feel because we don't want to disturb or distress them: we don't want to let them down. They don't want to see us struggle. It takes love, trust and confidence on the part of all to allow a situation to be faced and a solution to be found.

I am reminded of the story of a nun who was becoming more and more ill as a result of staying with her order. Finally it took a sensitive and caring community to suggest to her that she should, for her own sake, leave and make a new life for herself. She had taken life vows and could not bring herself to break them. She had given her life to God and believed that it would be a sin to leave, that she would be snatching back her offering made more than 30 years before. It would be a further three years before she moved out of the community into a property less than half a mile away: a place where she could feel secure yet free to be herself and to live without either the guilt of staying in the community, which she regarded as 'living under false pretences', or the guilt that had burdened her thoughts about leaving. She remained on excellent terms with the community. She recovered her health and found energy for creativity which brought in a modest income. Sometimes the most loving thing to do is to set someone free from their ministry. In such scenarios we discern the role of the Holy Spirit as gift and fruit of love, and as disturber and encourager.

When we consider what disturbs the calm waters of contentment, we recognize that disturbing the water is not like a sole swimmer doing a gentle breast stroke down the length of a swimming pool. If the Church could be thought of as a swimming pool it would be more like a public swimming bath on a Bank Holiday Monday: lots of people, some of whom can swim better than others. Some are more prepared to dive down and explore, others are content to float on the surface. We are all in the swim together and, while we might support each other, sometimes we are also likely to bump into each other. Calm waters can be difficult to find! Making a retreat, taking time out for rest and refreshment, making space in the day for stillness before God are ways of seeking a little still water in which to be bathed by God and be content in the presence of God. But we cannot dwell there permanently, never to engage with the world and the life of the family, of the Church. Continual reference to God in contemplation should always lead to reflection on God's mission. The spirit of God urges us to move from pious introspection to prayerful service of God and humankind. How important it is to sustain a balance of prayerful reflection, of worship and adoration of God with mission-oriented service! Even those called to contemplative religious life do not lose sight for a moment of the missionary context of a life of prayer.

This balance is essential to a healthy spirituality and places us in a good position to heed the call of the Spirit to a transition in ministry. Rolheiser (1998) describes what he regards as 'the essentials of a Christian spirituality – the four non-negotiable pillars of the spiritual life'. He regards them as undergirding any healthy Christian spirituality. They resonate with an understanding of 'tension' or 'balance' between attendance upon God and attention to the needs of the world. The four 'pillars' Rolheiser describes are:

1. private prayer and private morality
2. social justice
3. mellowness of heart and spirit and
4. community as a constitutive element of true worship.

If we try to separate these components, we descend into a valley of spiritual disconnectedness leaving us somewhere between the landmark of the things of God and the landmark of the world in which we live. From the bottom of this valley it is difficult to see the view: the way ahead. Which of us has not spent some time in the valley of spiritual disconnectedness? Fortunately, our Lord, our supreme example of divine and human connectedness, meets us there and leads us out of the valley to vistas that can leave us breathless with delight.

Perhaps our propensity to separate the spiritual from the material has been learned or coloured by Paul's teaching on body and spirit (1 Thess. 5.23). A separation of the things of the spirit from the things of the flesh, rendering almost everything, except prayer, to the flesh. Rowan Williams (in Waller and Ward, 1999, p. 2) suggests that it is fairly clear from the rest of St Paul's work that 'spirit' is very far from being simply an area of human experience or a portion of the human constitution. He goes on to say that the major epistles make it plain that 'living in or according to the "spirit" is a designation of the entire set of human relations, to God and each other and our environment'.

However one reads the apostle Paul on this matter, there is an interconnectedness between the life we live and the God in whose Spirit we live it. We may assume that the seeker after an authentic spirituality has a belief in God, but we would need to ask what kind of God the seeker believes in. Where there is a declared understanding of Jesus as the Son of God, as the God-made-flesh, as the one who has revealed to us the nature of God, the seeker will need to have come to understand that the incarnation and resurrection of Jesus has implications for us all of a hallowing of humanity subsequently infused with the Spirit of God, and a need to hold in tension the transcendent and the immanent God. There can only be an authentic Christian spirituality where there is a theology, and spirituality is rooted and grounded in God and God is to be found revealed in humanity.

Appreciating the connection between God and humankind makes it easier to connect God's mission and the message of the gospel with the task of the Church. Every transition in ministry has to be understood as the Church adjusting continually to its understanding of its mission in the world and making the most of its ministerial resources. Many able writers have written about the relationship between God's will and the Church's task of deploying ministerial resources. Cocksworth and Brown (2002), Carr (1985), Croft (1999) and Giles (2006) are among those who offer insights into an approach to ministry under a disposition to be part of God's mission to the world, there being no discontinuity between that disposition as sensed and articulated in the early days of exploration of vocation at parish or diocesan level and the tenor of that disposition as carried into ministry.

Vision and dreams

The Holy Spirit is to be found, too, in vision and dreams. There are many instances in Scripture where God's people have been inspired by a vision or a dream. Sometimes what comes to fruition bears little resemblance to the original inspiration. As ideas are shaped into plans and action they are influenced by the vision and dreams of others whose expertise is employed, or whose advice is sought. How wonderfully the will of God can be revealed when the Body of Christ functions well!

When it comes to forwarding the Kingdom of God it is vital that God's people dare to dream dreams: even seemingly preposterously expansive dreams. How important it is that we encourage one another to be visionary, to help each other to discern the voice of God in such vision and to share the possibilities in that vision rather than to dismiss them out of hand. Sometimes, however, our dreams are not about the Kingdom of God but about the kingdom we wish to build for ourselves. When we listen to each other's vision of 'castles in the air', we gently ask each other 'whose kingdom is to be built here?' Having said that, one marvels at how a selfishly motivated dream, one that seems more self-serving that God-serving can become the launch pad of an adventure that brings about a glorious work for God.

Is it really that simple?

Stories such as those we have heard so far can inspire and encourage us but they can also make us ask ourselves a few questions. Is it really that simple? Are motives that pure? If we unpack our motives for even the most worthy of enterprises we will find that something of them is about ourselves: our reputation, our satisfaction or our gain. God is not proud! He accepts the less worthy elements of our endeavours and brings life and wholeness out of them for the good of others, for the good of the Kingdom. Some enterprises, entered into with the best of motives are wrought in us, heated and hammered into shape by God's Spirit. Visions become plans and actions through hard work, struggle, and by overcoming seemingly immovable obstacles. The joy of the out-come belies the pain, suffering, rows and arguments, disap-pointments, frustrations, rejections, tears and near despair that characterized the steps that led to the fulfilment of the dream.

When we listen to someone's story of how their dream became reality, we may only hear their version of it. We may not know how their achievement affected those around them. We can only imagine the impact on those who helped to shape the outcome or who paid dearly in the service of the dream. The danger of under-taking a largely phenomenological study of this kind is that we hear the world view of the storytellers, but we don't hear, for the most part, the view of the other stakeholders in a situation. What might be the truth of the story we hear? Where was God in the enterprise? Swinton and Mowat (2006) suggest a middle ground approach: a suspension of shared reality until proven otherwise, a hermeneutic of suspicion regarding the possibility of discover-ing shared truth. 'Then, through a careful process of observation, interpretation and analysis, move toward clearer and clearer *ap-proximations* of the truth' (p. 170). We stand between an epis-temology of informed experience and a position of received and conditioned faith constructs. In order to reconcile the two we may need those who support us to stand with us, taking co-ownership of the dilemma and seeking truth with us. Together we are on a truth-seeking mission and we seek the truth of our vocation in the heart of God's mission in the world. We find out what God is doing in a place or a circumstance and we offer to join in (Hey-wood, 2011). But what is God doing, how actively involved is God? What we hold to be true is that God is turning darkness to light, conflict to peace, hate to love. We ask ourselves if what we propose to do is going to work with God's mission to transform the world in love, peace and light.

Continual reference back to the source of all vision keeps the vision vibrant and purposeful. Belief in God empowers the vision and the outworking of the vision challenges belief. Our vision may have come out of what we believe about God, but our experi-ence of God and the outworking of our vision may well reshape what we believe about God! Referencing the vision to changing circumstances requires regular reflection on the nature of our call. We ask ourselves if what God wanted then is what God wants now. We consider how we have been changed by our experience of God and how our understanding of God may be different. We consider what we have learned about ourselves and about how God is at work in the world around us. We ask what the Church needs of us now compared to then. Out of such questions may come new vision, fresh ideas for how we might develop our relationship with God in prayer and in the service of our neighbour. Those responsible for discerning with us as we make a transition in ministry hope to find us growing in confidence and in the ability to reflect in this way: a practice of theological and spiritual reflection is a life-long exercise.

Dewar (2000) challenges his readers to consider the possibility that the average ordinand has not really reflected, at all, on their sense of call. He declares (p. 72) that from the answers ordinands and would-be ordinands have given to his questions he has the impression that most of them have not done any work at all on personal calling. He says that ordinands and would-be ordinands assume, in a lazy kind of a way, that they are called to be ordained, but he implies that their reflection takes them no further than that. He continues:

> A few of my respondents articulated a genuine enthusiasm for some task that obviously connected with their own needs, but it seemed they had not thought about it in terms of what God might be calling them to offer to *others*. Many described activities that they enjoyed, but most of these were of the ready-made variety, filling pre-existent slots of one kind or another, and nearly all of these were churchy slots. I am not trying to be unkind or rude in pointing all this out, just provocative. I think the whole Church needs waking up about the business of personal calling, and therefore would-be ordinands and their mentors do too. If the future clergy and leaders of the Church have not done any work on it, God help the rest of us!

I have to say that this has not been my experience. Ordinands and ministers in general do reflect deeply on their personal initial and on-going call, but they are not likely to make it the subject of general conversation. To do so at every turn would be to turn attention to ourselves. Sharing deeply of a personal call has value as witness to the grace and goodness of God, as a public act of gratitude, as an encouragement to those exploring their own call, but it is too precious a perfume to be sprayed willy nilly into the air.

Ordinands being formed by theology and experience

For the reader experienced in ministry there may be value in an anamnesis of our own early formational deliberation. We may ask ourselves if the exercises in discernment undertaken in early formation were just for then or whether they have become tools for continuing formation, in conformation to Christ and to the service of his Church.

Does the following scenario sound familiar? Does it resonate still? Ordinands, at the time of their decision making about a curacy, are likely to be somewhere between the theological, ecclesiological and cultural conditioning that had brought them into training and the 'owning' of theological constructs and ecclesiological variations on a theme that make ordinand life both exciting and scary. They experiment with models of theological reflection, comparing and contrasting them with models that they had previously used, implicitly or explicitly, as they journeyed to this time of intense learning. They draw on many fields and disciplines and survey a rainbow of theological sub-disciplines. Their own reflections and those of their guides and tutors become a reflective interplay, a critical conversation (Pattison 2000, p. 136, in Thompson et al., 2008) from which can come greater insight and learning for all involved. Ordinands' theological reflection is not just an exercise in theory: it has a practical application. More than that, it is the acquisition of a habit that is intended to underpin their lifelong ministerial praxis. Theological reflection is not meant as a cage to constrain growth towards God and the discernment of God's activity in the world: rather theological reflection is a climbing frame designed to aid growth and to facilitate a better 'view' of what is going on. When we are in the process of making a discerned decision about a transition in ministry, do we find it natural to employ reflective theological models to aid the process? A key point about ordinands deliberating about the transition into ordained ministry and the securing of a curacy is that much of the decision making takes place quite early in training when some ordinands are still trying to comprehend what theological reflection is! Are we better placed than they when it comes to later transitions in ministry?

Lest we think that theological reflection is the pastime only of the ordinand suspended from reality in the 'ivory tower' of a ministerial training programme it is worth reminding ourselves that the practice of theological reflection has, for some years now, been at the heart of all training for ordination, of lay reader training and, increasingly, is appearing on the syllabuses of lay training programmes throughout the Church. Sitting comfortably at the heart of practical theology, theological reflection keeps together reflection on God, the practices of the Church and those of the world at large. Practical theology has been described by Swinton and Mowat (2006, p. 6), as 'critical, theological reflection on the practices of the Church as they interact with the practices of the world, with a view to ensuring and enabling faithful participation in God's redemptive practices in, to and for the world'. The questions we ask ourselves as we contemplate a transition in ministry are the very questions the practical theologian asks. We ask questions about God, life and ourselves. Such questions may be new or different from many of those with which we have previously engaged, or they may be the same old questions newly contextualized. We bring these questions to bear upon a discerned decision-making process and we may emerge with new theological insights. From new theological insights there could be a fresh understanding of how to respond to God. Out of our dilemma can come new questions about God, questions and insights from deep within the practicalities of the life-context in which we next find ourselves. Veling (2005, p. 6) alludes to this:

[P]ractical theology suggests that we cannot separate knowing from being, thinking from acting, theological reflection from pastoral and practical involvement. Theology is always shaped by and embodied in the practices of historical, cultural and linguistic communities. Our understandings always emerge from our practices, or from the forms of life in which we participate.

When we recall the early stages of our own ministerial formation, we may not recall specific models of theological reflection. We may remember only nervousness, bewilderment and unknowing. Such phenomena still have their place! Might we not admit that those same phenomena are in evidence at every stage of ministry? Transitions in ministry are 'in-between' stages of ministry and bring their own characteristic concerns, anxieties, strengths, weaknesses, opportunities and threats. In our confusion and amid the cacophony of voices firing at us advice and information we may find ourselves asking, 'What is going on?' Standing at the centre of the maelstrom of a dilemma we may not be able to be totally objective. Realistically, we oscillate between moments of absolute clarity about what is going on and lengthy periods of opacity. Everything can appear flocculent, complex, and transitional.

Inspirational role models

These deliberations may help us to know ourselves a little better; what motivates us, what leads us on. We may also ask ourselves who else is like us, who inspires us and whom do we emulate. How the Christian life is lived will depend upon many factors. Many people will develop a 'style' of spirituality that resonates with what they know or have been taught about God or what they have learned about the spiritual 'greats' in every generation, all of whom will have modelled their life on that of Jesus Christ, who models for us the life of God in Trinity (Sykes in Waller and Ward, 1999).

Vision of our own becoming

In the search for the right next move we may look for signs that the ministry we are exploring has the potential to enable us to become the kind of minister we long to be. We picture ourselves in the role, doing the tasks that would befall us. We imagine the difference we might make: the contribution we might make to the building of the Kingdom of God. Where do those imaginings come from? For some they will have been inspired by role models: characters from the Scriptures, from Church history or people whom we have known and who have been part of our journey to this point, with Christ as our supreme role model whose ministry we not only emulate but in which we participate. A prayer attributed to Teresa of Avila says it so well:

Christ has no body now on earth but yours,
no hands but yours, no feet but yours,
yours are the eyes through which Christ's compassion
is to look out to the earth,
yours are the feet by which He is to go about doing good
and yours are the hands by which He is to bless us now.

Essentially, we need no other role model than that of the Lord, but other role models, especially those who also sought to model their own ministry on that of Jesus, may inspire us. Jesus was fully human and yet without sin. Sinful and human role models can seem a bit more like us. In the same way that a great explorer or adventurer may have been inspired, perhaps as a child, by stories of derring-do, so might we in the infancy of our Christian discipleship have been inspired by the heroes and heroines of our faith. The syllabus of our ministerial training will have, at the very least, touched upon martyrs, saints, reformers, teachers and other exemplars. Have we never said to ourselves: 'I would like to be like that person'? For example, Mother Theresa of Calcutta (1910–97) had been inspired by her own heroes of the faith and, in her turn, she became an inspiration not only to the sisters of her order but to countless people around the world. She demonstrated that you don't have to be dead to be a saint. What she models, and others like her, is the presence of Christ. They model this by who they are, by how they live, and by what they do in the service of others.

One meets ordinands and clergy who have looked to literature for role models, comparing and contrasting what they have read with their own lives and experience. They cite classic works, such as those by Benedict, Augustine, Thomas á Kempis, Ignatius of Loyola and George Herbert, all of whom have woven their own threads into the Church's rich tapestry. Some have been moved or inspired by more recent iconic figures such as Michael Ramsey and W. H. Vanstone. We may cite Giles (2006) and Carr (1985) as well as Cocksworth and Brown (2002), Pritchard (2007), Dewar (2000) and Witcombe (2005) as having influenced us, as well as other contemporary writers. Many such characters offer models of pastoral ministry which we may seek to employ. Some traditional models are being challenged, their relevance for contemporary ministry questioned. Perhaps we have learned either to love George Herbert or have come, with Lewis-Anthony (2009), to a desire to 'kill him'!

Percy (2006) demonstrates, comprehensively, how clergy have evolved as a 'species'. Will we encounter in ministry the same 'species' as we believe ourselves to be, and is that always a good thing? We are likely to compare our own ministerial style to that of others and, with a stronger contemporary emphasis on collaborative ministry, we are likely to compare our own style with that of the clergy with whom we are expected to collaborate. Perhaps we will discern God-givenness in the complementarity of the styles of potential colleagues, and be able to celebrate our difference. When considering a move there will be questions like 'Will I fit in?' to a wider ministerial context, not forgetting that the ministerial team we are considering joining will be asking themselves if we will fit in with them!

History offering glimpses of life ahead

For those setting out in ministry, reading of the experiences of both historic and contemporary ministers offers glimpses of what may lie ahead. When someone says: 'I just want to give my life to God,' it would be unusual for them to refer, at that point, to the possibility of martyrdom, yet, potentially, that is what giving one's life to God might entail. We are more likely to mean that we are prepared to make the service of God and the proclamation of the gospel our life's work, without thought to the potentially life-threatening consequences of doing so. Some things are easy to say if the context of that lived life presents few life-threatening challenges, but the search for illumination and for insight into how sacrificial ministry might be experienced takes both the would-be minister, and those making further transitions in ministry, on a mental tour of the experience of those who have gone before us.

Those who have inspired us in our own faith journey, both contemporary and iconic ministerial ancestors, are a source of wisdom to us. We seek to see life and ministry through their eyes, through their hearts, their hands, their feet. The writer of the letter to the Hebrews (11.32–end) refers the reader to such exemplars of faith and sacrifice, citing graphically the price they paid for their devotion to God and the gospel. Do we glimpse their fate from the corner of our eye as we focus our attention on God and his mission?

Teachers of the faith lay upon us constructs of God and give us creedal statements to learn by rote, but confessors of the faith give us a glimpse of what God is like. They encourage us to look around us for the presence of God, to find him in human experience, in daily life. Life circumstances and human suffering (our own or that of others) can cause us to reconstruct our thinking about what God is like. We may move, because of life experience, from an acceptance of the faith statements we were taught as non-negotiable definitions of the Christian faith, to new insights into God or the personhood of Jesus Christ or the nature of the Church. We find it is possible to start with experience and to ask ourselves what it has taught us about the nature of God.

Not knowing God, yet having him revealed to us in Jesus Christ and knowing his presence in the Holy Spirit is a liberating paradox. Esther de Waal (1989, p. 33) suggests that '[w]e are all people of paradox. Each of us knows only too well the conflicting claims of child and adult, of male and female, of animus and anima, of heart and head.'

She asserts that:

> Living with paradox may well not always be easy or comfortable. It is not something for the lazy, the complacent, the fanatical. It does however point us the way to truth and life. For as we learn to live with paradox we have to admit that two realities may be equally true; we may be asked to hold together contrasting forces. The closer we come to saying something worthwhile, the more likely it is that paradox will be the only way to express it. The mind will never apprehend the truth of paradox. Only the heart can do that.

She goes on to remind us of some of the paradoxical elements of our faith: 'a God who becomes man; a victor who rides on a donkey in his hour of triumph'. She continues that the ultimate paradox of life through death is a paradox which can only be lived, and she concludes that 'the promise is that we shall learn to live with contradiction, holding together the tensions in such a way that we will let them become creative and life-enhancing for us' (de Waal, 1989, p. 22).

It is seductive to think that such wisdom and insight can only come with age or life-experience. Here we recognize something more of paradox: the older we get the more we realize how little we know or understand. Life is not about finding answers to questions so much as finding out what questions to ask. There is no correlation between the number of years we have spent in ministry and the resolution or acceptance of mystery. How humbling it is to be working among wise young (and not so young) owlets preparing for ordained ministry, who know and own both their knowledge and their ignorance!

Testimony to the power of prayer

There is a flaw in a logical and reasoned approached to discerned decision making. That flaw is the intervention or the interaction of God in the process. It is the unexpected turn of events: the meeting of a stranger whose casual remark changes our perception of what a transition might be about. It is the opening of doors we thought were shut for ever. It is the sudden and inexplicable removal of an obstacle in the pathway of a dream. It is the answer to prayer.

The Spirit of God blows where it will (John 3.8). Sometimes it is a gentle breeze that wafts around us bringing comfort in the heat of a dilemma, and sometimes it is a gale-force wind that lifts us off our feet and brings us down again in an unfamiliar place. The Spirit of God disturbs the calm waters of complacency and carries us on a tide of inspiration into uncharted waters, into a new adventure. When considering a transition in ministry, the Spirit of God asks only that we allow ourselves to be carried on the tide to the place of possibility. In Chapter 3 we consider the God-givenness of the maps and compasses we use to guide us through transition, the devices we employ to help us to make our navigational decisions.

3

How We Make Decisions

'Do you want the job or not? Yes or no!' asked the Diocesan Director of Ordinands (DDO) of the procrastinating would-be curate. 'Yes and no', he replied.

There are times when procrastinators need help in the form of a deadline for making a decision. Taking overlong to decide on a job offer causes problems for all the stakeholders in the appointment process, as well as for other candidates who have been considered or to whom an invitation might subsequently be made. Having said that, as we reflect on how people make decisions, we could usefully unpack the brief exchange quoted above and ask ourselves a few questions: 'Are all decisions, ultimately, a matter of saying "yes *or* no"?' The second question is: 'Is the answer, "yes *and* no" solely about procrastination or can we hear in the sigh that accompanies the delivery, something deeper, something, mystical?' Is it not more likely that, in every decision, there is a 'no' which correlates with a 'yes'?

When Jesus called his first disciples with the invitation: 'Follow me' (Matt. 4.18,19), there was a 'yes' to following Jesus and a 'no' to being a fisherman, to being a family man, to the routine of daily life. When the Archangel Gabriel invited the Blessed Virgin Mary to be the mother of the Lord, he waited for her fiat. Heaven held its breath until she said 'yes', because she could have said 'no'. If she did not have that choice, the unwanted invasion of her body would have been tantamount to rape. If she had said 'no', she would have been saying 'yes' to the life lived by other young women in her society, and we would never have known of her.

The option of 'no' is vital to decision making, as vital as the option of 'yes'. Either may allow something wonderful to happen.

Saying 'no' is very difficult for a lot of people and accounts for many problems in life. Confining our reflection to the experience of ordained ministry, one comes across ministers who cannot say no and so get overwhelmed by all they have agreed to do. Some ministers regard the unequivocal 'yes' as the very core of their vocation. They view it as the essence of servanthood, but is it not more like slavery? Does it not encourage exploitation by others and, at some level, does it not feed a need in the minister rather than answer the need of those they seek to serve?

In the course of a day we make hundreds of decisions. Plotted on a chart they are a binary account of all that we do. There are many uses of the term 'binary'. It is used in chemistry, engineering, astronomy and social sciences. Mathematicians use the term for the binary numbering system which is central to computer technology. Binary numbers only make sense when 'zero' and 'one' are used, one with the other, in a variety of combinations. I am old enough to remember a precursor to the modern computer that used punch cards to send information. In a specific place on the card, there was either a hole or there wasn't. The holes were of equal value to the spaces, because it was the sequence of holes and spaces which relayed the information. It is the same with 'yes' and 'no'. They are equally important in the dialogue of life. Both responses can bring life to a circumstance. Saying 'yes' to the life-giving grace of God has its corollary in saying 'no' to life-taking sin. But how would a theologian use the term 'binary'? Responding 'yes and no' may not always be about procrastination so much as an awareness of the consequences of a 'yes' or 'no' response: the implications of a response in one direction bringing equal awareness of the implications of its corollary.

This brings to mind the writing of the Swiss theologian, Karl Barth who, in his great work, *Church Dogmatics* (1960, pp. 296–7), writes about the 'yes' and 'no' of creation. He suggests that for God to create all things out of nothing, nothingness had to exist and that

> [w]hen Jesus Christ shall finally come as the Lord and Head of all that God has created, it will also be revealed that both in light and shadow, on the right hand and on the left, everything created was very good and supremely glorious.

He goes on to comment that

> It is true that in creation there is not only a Yes but also
> a No; not only a height but also an abyss; not only clarity
> but also obscurity; not only progress and continuation but
> also impediment and limitation; not only growth but also
> decay . . .

Barth breaks off from his discourse on creation with the inter-
position, on pages 297–9, of a discourse about theophonic revelation he hears in Mozart's music, recognizing his compositions as
a conduit for this paradox of the revelation of Jesus Christ as the
eternal 'yes' and 'no' of God. My poem below was inspired by
Barth's postulation:

'Yes' and 'No'

Holy, wholly Other, Being;
yet in Jesus Christ revealing!
Some, like Barth, have said it's so;
between Creation and Chaos propounding
(insouciant Mozart dark-light sounding?)
theories of God's 'Yes' and 'No'.

Jesus, Word, quite contrary;
how you let your people go!
With wood and nails
and wondrous tales
of love and judgement:
a paradox of 'Yes' and 'No'.

To the darkest place descending;
where the morbid souls did go,
eternal grief and death expecting
or relief awaiting – gently resting?
Jesus Christ, in love is raising;
speaking to them of 'Yes' and 'No'.

God the Father in glory reigning,
his victorious Son to show;
through his Spirit; how reflecting
to show the way the world should go;
to be faithful to all his teaching
in his eternal 'Yes' and 'No'.

The 'yes' and 'no' of creation is modelled in the story of Adam and Eve. Esther de Waal (1989, p. 24), comments on their decision to cover their nakedness with fig leaves (Gen. 3.7). She comments:

Here is a split within themselves, for when they cover their nakedness with leaves they are rejecting their original wholeness. Their subsequent argument as to whose fault it was that they had eaten the forbidden fruit brought about a split in their relationship and their resultant expulsion from the Garden of Eden brought about a split with the environment.

De Waal highlights how the decisions we make, how splits brought about by disobedience, by a decision made contrary to the will of God, have eternal consequences. She describes how a choice of words can dishonour another and how a lifestyle choice can be bruising to the environment with far-reaching consequences.

Being caught somewhere between two choices, to say 'yes' or 'no', to accept or to reject, does not feel like a blessed space in which to lounge or linger! It can be an agonizing place to dwell. Sometimes choices are not between good and evil so much as between a greater or lesser evil or good. We can long for a quick and easy resolution, but we may be no better off, no more at peace about a decision made in haste. Depending on time pressures we may find that to sit with a decision, to pray with a decision, seeking the wisdom of God, raises a third option: a better option than either of those with which we have wrestled.

There is, of course, a time-honoured way of making a decision. We call it 'the toss of a coin', but what kind of decisions would we trust to such a decision-making device, and can God's will be made known that way? Do Christians subscribe to this method of making decisions? Is the random consultation of the Bible the nearest equivalent? Jackson (cited by Martin, 1990, p. 13) describes how he and his wife reached a decision about a house to rent for the duration of a proposed curacy, a house they considered to be too nice for them. They opened a Bible at a random page and found an affirmative answer on the page before them! It was 'Remain in the house, eating and drinking what they provide, for the labourer deserves his wages; do not go from house to house' (Luke 10.7). Jackson writes, however, about the generous and warm hospitality shown them by the house owners. Was the scriptural text that 'spoke' to them merely a more culturally acceptable basis for saying 'yes' than simply the rather more human experience of warm hospitality?

We look for devices to help us make decisions using a binary approach to two equally attractive or unattractive options. I am grateful to a good friend of mine who shared an account of a decision about a move in ministry recorded in the diaries of his late father (let us call him David). This story might serve to illustrate how a godly person seeking the will of God used a binary approach to decision making. While in his thirties and serving as a Presbyterian minister, David was invited by a chapel on the west coast of Wales to 'preach with a view'. The invitation was warm and positive, and he sensed that if he were to preach with a view it was likely that he would be invited to become their minister. As he was considering this invitation, another arrived in the form of a telephone call from a friend in Manchester. The friend spoke animatedly about a plan to establish a chapel in a needy part of the city. The friend was certain that David was just the man for the job!

David now found himself with a dilemma. There were attractions to both places. Both would draw on his energy, strengths and gifts. Both involved a relocation with much in the area to commend it. He prayed and sought God's will, but his dilemma was unresolved and he could not leave both invitations indefinitely unanswered. What should he do? He decided to write a letter to the West Wales chapel committee thanking them for their invitation and stating that he would be pleased to come and preach with a view. He addressed the envelope, sealed it and put a stamp on it. Then he wrote another letter. Again, this was addressed to the West Wales chapel committee, but this time he wrote thanking them for their invitation but stating that he was considering another direction for his ministry. As before, he addressed and sealed the envelope and put a stamp on it. He put both envelopes in his jacket pocket and walked to the post box. Then, without looking, he took out one of the envelopes and dropped it in the letter-box. Subsequently he preached with a view at the West Wales chapel and was invited to be their minister. He had a very fruitful ministry there that included making links with a nearby university and a role in the training of other ministers.

David took the initiative to do something rather than do nothing. He would have had a fruitful ministry wherever he had gone. He had sought God's guidance and if he had been subject to a higher earthly authority he may well have sought their advice and gone, in obedience, to the ministry they thought most appropriate for him at that time. His decision then would have been to obey rather than to disobey. In the end there is a decision that no one else can make. We have to take responsibility both for our choice of decision-making methodology and for the decisions we make.

Decisions in time and space: Rachel's helpful day

Rachel had been considering whether or not she was called to ordained ministry. She pondered, too, on what kind of ordained ministry she might be called to exercise. She tells how she went on a 'Day of Reflection' and how something became clear to her for the very first time. She had been greatly inspired by three points made by the event leader. These were:

1. I can only discern for me.
2. I can only discern for now.
3. I can only discern what might be good.

She commented: 'I realize that I have to trust my own sense of discernment too. I think I have been trying to rely on other people discerning for me.' Up to this point Rachel had relied heavily on other people's opinion of whether or not she was called to ordained ministry. Her assumption had been that if everyone else thought so, then it must be so, whether or not she was convinced for herself. She continued: 'I think part of me has been trapped inside a teenage mindset from which I am being released and moving into a more adult way of thinking . . . at the age of 45! When I think back to being 18, I didn't feel able to make a choice about my future and relied very heavily on the guidance of others. At that point I didn't have a desire to follow any particular career path, all I wanted was to be married and have children, and if that didn't happen then to devote my whole life to God and be a nun!'

A change of mindset had begun to emerge before the workshop as it became clear to Rachel that she did not feel called to run a parish. She had begun to articulate what, within ordained ministry, she could say 'yes' to and what she should say 'no' to. Owning our own decisions in discernment is as important as taking into account the opinions of others. A call to ministry is always to be discerned corporately within the Church as the Body of Christ, but does not exclude our own discernment on the matter.

When considering the 'now' of discernment we not only avoid looking too far ahead, but we shake off the old 'us' and our perceptions of who we used to be. We ask ourselves who we are now and we ponder on who we might become. Rachel is right to remember that she is a 45 year old woman making this discerned decision and that she has life experience and wisdom to bring to bear on it. Rachel was also encouraged by the third of the three points raised by the day of reflection. She gained a deeper understanding that 'doing what might be good' invites a testing of what is good and wholesome: what is holy and what will honour God.

Ordinands' approach to decision making

Although a decision has to be made 'for now' it does not rule out the journey up to now. Continually looking back and looking forward, scanning experience and imagination, is another binary dimension to decision making. This happens throughout our ministry but can be clearly seen in the decision making of ordinands who stand at the threshold of ministry. Some have unresolved issues about the rightness, for them, of becoming ordained and as they wrestle with those unresolved issues the clock is ticking, the proposed date of their ordination approaches and there is a decision to be made about a title post. They look back at a work and lifestyle they have left behind, a world they knew and understood. They look forward to a world they have yet to understand or to experience fully.

That is not the only axis of reflection. They explore, too, the validation of their own experience over and against the faith constructs they have received: always a dilemma for the fledgling practical theologian. Do they rely on what they know or do they trust to what they do not yet know? Some have had many years experience of secular models of decision making but is that experience of any value to them in the dilemma before them?

The role of intuition

One of the Cuddesdon Twelve remarked how his decision-making style had changed over the years and how he was now more likely to trust his intuition. But what is intuition? Hayashi (2001, p. 61) quotes Henry Mintzberg, Professor of Management at McGill University and 'a long-time proponent of intuitive decision making', who asserts that intuition is 'the sense of revelation at the obvious (which) occurs when one's conscious mind finally learns something that one's subconscious mind had already known'. This we could term 'tacit knowledge' or intuition. Most of the Cuddesdon Twelve respondents referred, in one form or another, to this as being part of their discerned decision making. A few even suggested that the 'voice' of intuition and the 'voice' of God are one and the same thing. They tended to use the word 'intuition' and 'instinct' interchangeably. Hayashi (p. 64) warns, however, that instincts can be wrong, that we may see patterns where none exist and do what statisticians call 'over fitting the data'.

One respondent had always relied on his instincts when making secular business decisions and had applied that same instinct in accepting a curacy, but felt that he 'got it wrong'. It could be said that intuition is informed by experience and knowledge and the respondent had only that which he brought with him from secular employment, and now his more recently informed intuition told him he 'got it wrong'.

One size does not fit all!

Among the Cuddesdon Twelve respondents there were replicable patterns and commonalities in approach to decision making but there was also a significant individualistic dimension to the process: it is about one unique ordinand settling effectively into one title post. Can there be, therefore, a 'blueprint' for how to approach this stage of ordained ministry since those called are unique and the context of their ministry unique? Cocksworth and Brown (2002, p. 4) suggest that 'the permutations are affected by any number of psychological, social, economic, theological and cultural factors that render futile any attempts to offer a blueprint for ministry regardless of the particularities of personality, place, position'. Cocksworth and Brown acknowledge, however, that there are 'certain conditions, characteristics and consequences of an ordained life that stand in common across the centuries, cultures and contexts'.

All these factors comprise the milieu in which we make a discerned decision about a transition in ministry. The curacy decision, however, has one significant difference: the limitation of choice by the absence of concurrent options of curacy vacancies and offers. Gross (2001, p. 300) argues that this approach to decision making inhibits rationality, reduces effectiveness and leaves the problem-solver with a heuristic approach. But is trial and error an option here? Many believe that it would be both undesirable and unworkable to have ordinands competing for curacy vacancies and that it might lead to a kind of 'market economy' mentality where parishes would seek to attract 'the best' ordinand.

No great regret was expressed by the Twelve respondents that only one curacy vacancy is offered at a time, but most expressed the view that it did heighten concern about turning down the first or even the second offer, even if there were serious reservations about it. In some instances a first offer had been accepted, because it had been intimated that there would be no other offer. Overall the respondents had given the decision about a curacy considerable thought and they were optimistic about the future.

Although the curate/incumbent relationship emerged from the research as the most important issue, several respondents had accepted a curacy offer with serious doubts about the outworking of that relationship because they were concerned that they would 'end up with nothing'. In some instances this decision had made for lamentable consequences. It is worth noting that two out of six curate respondents had reported experiencing significant difficulties and that one of the curacies seemed likely to end disastrously (subsequently the curate had to move). This indicates the need for a culture of openness, not of fear, if curacy placements are to be more fruitful. It is not acceptable to suggest that God can bring good things out of our mistakes (as one respondent reasoned). Of course he can, but that is not a good reason not to strive to get it right in the first place: and that may require a reappraisal of the skills, gifts and competences of all those involved in the process.

Secular authorities on decision making in organizations

In order to address the question of how people make effective decisions I turned to authorities in secular organizational fields, in part because many of those who are making discerned decisions have been schooled in secular decision-making models prior to embarking on ordained ministry and continue to employ them, and also to appraise what secular models may have to offer. How then do organizations make effective decisions?

Anecdotal evidence suggests that the decision-making process cannot be described in solely objective terms. In supporting this view, Heller (1998) is not making a pejorative statement, rather a statement of fact. This view allows for the validity of intuition and for data that cannot be measured: a cross-referencing of data open to the influence of experience and acquired wisdom. Peter F. Drucker, who created the Foundation for Nonprofit Management, has written and taught, and has counselled numerous governments, businesses and public service institutions. He asserts (2001) that the world of business and commerce did not invent decision-making models, rather they adopted them, based on many years of social science research into how people make effective decisions.

Those who argue that the world of business and commerce has no place in the Church may recognize that Christians in secular employment use such adopted methods and that such people can be found in decision-making bodies within the life of the Church: from the Archbishops' Council, through General Synod, to the local parochial church council (PCC). The question before us is whether models of effective decision making adopted by church officers and sourced from the collective experience of decision making (within or without the church) are applicable to decision making in transitions in ministry.

We live in a secular world. It is largely where we minister and where we engage with secular organizations and culture, and we are capable of reconciling both secular and ecclesiastical decision-making practices. We may find that the ethos or values of some secular organizations are more closely identifiable with the Church than others: the charitable and public sector, for example. Other organizations may bring us greater challenge if their ethos seems counter-culture: for example in the world of business and commerce. It is not that we dismiss secular decision-making constructs out of hand, rather that we try to be discerning about their adoption. So, what do secular authorities have to offer us?

Secular decision-making theories

There is a plethora of relevant literature in the field of decision-making theory. The Harvard Business School has a whole faculty

dedicated to it. Such authorities offer an intellectual and pragmatic learning that could be of value to our reflections. Authors
concede, however, that while they have come up with models
that are elegant and effective, very few decision-makers actually
follow them! John S. Hammond (1999, p. 2), an internationally
known consultant, speaker and author, and a former professor
at the Harvard Business School, argues that decision making is
a life skill and that 'one can learn to make better decisions'. All
the literature I consulted suggests that decision making involves
a distinctive process. Individual authors offer similar frameworks
or key steps in that process, but each offers an authorial emphasis
or dimension. Heller (1998, p. 8), for example, offers a series of
questions as a work method for making a decision. Questions include: What exactly has to be decided? What are the alternatives?
What are the pros and cons? Which alternatives are best? What
action needs to be taken?

Butler and Hope (2007) suggest various techniques such as trial
runs and the need, when there are time pressures, to distinguish
the urgent from the important. Others draw on neuro-linguistic
programming techniques of imagining outcomes and planning
steps to the realization of a vision. Butler and Hope (p. 453) suggest that 'younger people are more influenced by immediate and
short-term considerations . . . older people find adaptation to
change harder to cope with . . . they need longer to make decisions'. Gross (2001, p. 300) on the heuristics in decision making
states that it is not always easy to make rational decisions, even in
important matters, because of the absence of information about
the various alternatives. There isn't always time to make a totally
rational decision, which adds yet more pressure. When all factors
are taken into consideration it is unlikely that we are ever able to
make a totally logical or rational decision.

Meyer and Hutchinson (in Hoch et al. [eds] 2001, p. 37), both
lecturers at the Wharton Business School in Pennsylvania, offer
a chapter on the science of what they call 'bumbling geniuses'
which takes a complex and algebraic route to say what Amitai
Etzioni, Ford Foundation Professor at Harvard Business School
from 1987 to 1989, and subsequently a professor at the George

Washington University, said more comprehensively in his 1989 article entitled, 'The science of muddling through' in the *Harvard Business Review*.

Many of these authorities work with executives in organizations, teaching how to improve decision-making skills. 'Executive' is a risky word to use in Church circles as it has a connotation of top-down power that we might like to think does not exist in the Church. We might prefer a 'bottom up' approach to things and will easily argue that Jesus is no 'Chief Executive'. Conscious of some resistance in the Church to the use of secular models and terminology, I would like to *borrow* the word 'executive' for the purposes of our reflection, as a term to mean 'one who makes a decision'. In the process of making a transition in ministry the minister is an executive, 'one who makes a decision', notwithstanding that others in the process (bishops, for example) will have an executive role with a connotation of seniority.

Authorities in decision-making theory assert that executives, when making decisions, embrace an organization's policies, protocols, procedures, ethics, aims and objectives. How is the Church different? A PCC, for example, when making decisions, may refer to a mission strategy, may be cognizant of canon or civil law as well as being constrained by legislation regarding health and safety or the disabilities discrimination acts.

Peter F. Drucker (2001, p. 1), argues that executives 'want to know what the decision is all about and what the underlying realities are which it has to satisfy': what a decision needs to achieve. These he calls 'boundary considerations'. He goes on:

> [E]ffective executives know when a decision has to be based on principle and when it should be made pragmatically, on the merits of the case. They know the trickiest decision is that between the right and the wrong compromise, and they have learned to tell one from the other. (p. 2)

Drucker warns against making the wrong kind of compromise when a solution does not seem to be entirely appropriate to the problem, and suggests that stakeholders should be clear about what is 'right' rather than what is acceptable before compromises, adaptations and concessions are made. He writes of two kinds of compromise: 'half a loaf is better than no bread' and the judgement of Solomon, where half a baby is worse than no baby at all! Drucker (2001) argues that the former is a more acceptable compromise ('there is food'), but we may want to say that the second, which involves sacrificial love, is a 'right' compromise. His use of a biblical story to illustrate his point is not lost on us. Drucker's central point is that one should not start with what is acceptable but with what is right (p. 13).

Hoch et al. (2001, flyleaf), drawing 'from several decades of research into the psychological, interactive and temporal aspects of decision making' and defending the need to learn how to make effective decisions, asserts that 'human beings are not well equipped to make the best decisions all or even most of the time' (p. 8) and that 'human beings do not, in general, follow logical models of choice' (p. 10). They comment that dilemmas of choice in the face of an uncertain and complex world have long been the focus of religion, literature and philosophy, but that it has not been until recently that decision making has been the subject of systematic investigation.

Drucker (2001) makes a distinctive contribution to a process-led approach to decision making by asking two key questions: Is the problem that needs to be solved generic, exceptional or unique? Is it a new genus for which no rule has yet been made? He further subdivides this question into two headings: (i) generic that is symptomatic – the problem is generic and (ii) a unique event for the individual or institution but which is actually generic. A decision about a transition in ministry could be said to be the latter: it is unique for the individual minister but generic for the diocese(s) within the genus of the Church. Does the decision then have to be treated as unique? The author asserts, however, that unique events are rare. Conversely, he warns the reader to beware of treating a new event as if it were just another example of an old problem.

Etzioni (1989, p. 123) offers a useful planning methodology. He suggests that people adopt one of three approaches to decision making. The first he describes as 'Incrementalism' or 'the science of muddling through' (p. 50). He states that incrementalism 'despairs of knowledge and instead concentrates on the smallest units of change without any sense of a grand design'. The second approach he describes as 'Rationalism': the gathering of data, facts, opinions and options before making a decision. He comments that rationalism has taught executives to expect more of themselves than is either possible or desirable, the implicit assumption being that decision-makers have unqualified power and wisdom when in possession of all the facts (p. 50). The third approach Etzioni describes as 'Humble decision making'. He describes this approach as proceeding with only partial information (which has not been fully processed or analysed) but with modest vision or sense of direction.

He allows a combination of these which he calls 'mixed scanning or adaptive (humble) decision making' which involves two sets of judgements. The first of these is located in broad, basic choices about an organization's goals and policies and the second is located in small, experimental decisions based on in-depth examination of a focused subset of facts and choices. Is this where we are lodged when making a decision about a transition in ministry?

Etzioni recognizes that decisions are likely to be both corporate and individual and suggests that 'successful decision-making strategies must necessarily include a place for co-operation, coalition building, and the whole panorama of differing personalities, perspectives, responsibilities and powers' (p. 123). He suggests that the main strengths of incrementalism are that it 'eliminates the need for complete encyclopaedic information' by focusing on limited areas: those nearest to hand, one at a time. It 'avoids the danger of grand policy decisions by not making any'. He goes on to comment that incrementalism is 'highly conservative and invariably chooses a direction close to the prevailing one with no radical change'. Commenting on the value of 'humble decision making', he remarks that it is not new but is well suited to modern times with the pressures of data overload (p. 123).

Alden Hayashi, Senior Editor of the *Harvard Business Review* (2001, p. 169) addresses the question of when it is appropriate to trust one's gut. He comments that 'many executives rely on intuition, gut instinct, hunches, inner voice but they cannot describe what they mean by that'. He presents research of leading scientists who suggest that our emotions and feelings may not only be important in our intuitive ability to make good decisions but may actually be essential. 'Specifically,' he continues, 'one theory contends that our emotions help us filter various options quickly, even if we are not consciously aware of the screening' (p. 59). It is interesting and reassuring to note that instinct and intuition have such value in the secular business world where one might suppose that 'hard fact' is the only currency of value.

We considered earlier that, sometimes, when a minister is making reference to 'instinct', 'intuition', or 'gut feeling' they are equating it directly with the promptings of the Holy Spirit. How does that compare then, with our own experience? What value do we place on instinct and intuition? At one level it might be only inarticulate reservation. At another level it may be the deep prompting of the Holy Spirit warning us to exercise caution or encouraging us to step out in faith, to go with our instinct in the absence of 'hard' evidence. Perhaps Susan's account of an incident early in the exploration of a curacy offer might help us here.

Susan's story

Susan parked her car a few hundred yards from the vicarage hoping the short walk would help to clear her head. She was to meet, for the first time, her prospective curacy training incumbent. She had doubts about the curacy in Moortown but could not articulate them. She hoped she would not make a fool of herself in front of the incumbent, and she hoped that her doubts would give way to certainty one way or the other. The incumbent turned out to be very pleasant: someone with whom she could work. All her queries were answered satisfactorily, but she still did not feel reassured about going to Moortown to serve her title. An hour and a quarter later, Susan walked back to her car. There, above and behind the car, was an enormous poster which read: 'Just say no!' Susan mused whether or not God would make his will known in this way. Did it seem an objective reason to give to those who awaited her decision? All Susan knew, at that point, was that she would turn down the offer of a curacy in Moortown but she still could not articulate the reasons why. Her instinct was to reject the offer even though she dreaded having to give a logical reason for her decision. The 'Just say no' sign, whether it was a valid sign from God or merely a coincidence, had nourished her instinctive reservation.

Susan came to realize that she would reject the offer because she could not bring herself to move 200 miles further away from her dependent parents. Her sponsoring bishop, while understanding her decision asked her to consider who, in the light of her entry into ordained ministry, were now her 'family'. Although Susan was subsequently offered a curacy in Neartown, just half an hour's drive from her parents' home, she carried a burden of guilt for having chosen to encompass her parents' needs in her discerned decision. Incidentally, the post at Moortown was filled almost immediately and the post-holder and benefice thrived.

Supposing there had been another poster in eye-view at the same time as the 'Just say no' poster and it had read 'Moortown needs you!' Would Susan have seen it? When we are conscious that our intuition is 'holding court' and virtually silencing the voices of logic, reason and practicality, we scan for supporting evidence, seeing signs in this and that occurrence, timing or event. The danger is that we will pick and choose phenomena which support what intuition is saying. Only with hindsight will we be able to say 'I was right to follow my instinct' or, 'I wish I had followed my instinct on that occasion.' Such deep reflection can be exhausting and rarely takes place outside the context of practical considerations, busyness and the solving of logistical problems, all of which can characterize a major change in ministry, lifestyle or relocation.

Scriptural warrant in the process of decision making

Many look to an Old and New Testament hermeneutic and to New Testament ecclesiology for authority, guidance and inspiration as they consider a transition in ministry. Some will regard specific scriptural warrant as critical to their decision making but there may be questions here about the use and abuse of the Bible. There is a difference between coming across a passage of Scripture that 'speaks' to us when we are seeking divine guidance and searching the Scriptures to find a passage which fits what we have already determined to do!

The Scriptures offer reference to how decisions relating to ministerial deployment were approached in the early days of the Church and many would argue that New Testament models still have much to teach. But is a twenty-first-century church likely to adhere to New Testament models given the continuing revision of how the church sets about ministry in the service of mission? If there are differences between historical and contemporary approaches to mission and ministry, might there be different approaches to discernment and to decision-making processes?

It is clear that discerned decision making does not take place in isolation. The corporate nature of transitions in ministry cannot be overemphasized and in this the experience of the New Testament Church may assist us. Kuhrt (2000, p. 89), referring to the selection of Matthias (Acts 1.20–26), states that a process was applied which featured scriptural guidance (v. 20), agreed selection criteria (vv. 21f), and the drawing up of a shortlist (v. 23). This was followed by prayer (v. 24f) and then by the drawing of lots (v. 26). The emphasis here is on a community engaged in discernment (Robinson and Wall 2006, p. 104): the individuals concerned seem to have little input in the matter! This process resembles the secular decision-making models we explored earlier that advocate reference to organizational ethos, aims and objectives (Scripture), person specification (criteria), a shortlist of candidates, consultation with senior executives (prayer?) and the selection of an appointee (drawing lots is sometimes not far from the truth!).

Implicit in the process of discernment is the weighing of many factors including reputation, ability and character. We would, perhaps, call it a 'reference'. Marshall (1980, p. 202), with regard to the sending of Barnabas and others to Antioch (Acts 15.22f), states that Barnabas had the complete confidence of Church authorities in Jerusalem because he was from a dispersion family. He was a pivot or link between Hebrew and Hellenistic elements of the Church, and he was highly suitable for the task. His human qualities were well known and there is no one else in Acts whom the author, Luke, describes as 'good'. Authorities attest to the spiritual insight of Barnabas: that his gifts were well suited to the needs of the growing Church at that time. Clearly, he was the right person for the job. A commission has to be accepted as well as given. What then, of Barnabas's response? It seems that it was generous and unequivocal.

There would seem to be an emphasis in the New Testament Church, not on a call to a specific place, but to a specific message (of salvation through repentance). In the sending out of the disciples (Luke 10.2), for example, Jesus does not offer a strategy for mission. Robinson and Wall (2006) offer reasoned arguments that the Church is not a democracy (p. 105), and yet one hears of ordinands entering into negotiations with diocesan authorities regarding a curacy offer as if the Church *were* a democracy. Robinson and Wall suggest that, in New Testament Church experience, the process begins not with the needs or aspirations of the individual, but with a community which hears of distress and frames the problem or challenge. The apostles provide guiding principles before giving the work back to the people with the problems. The community, with the apostles, discern the will of God and a public ritual marks the decision made. In all these accounts the apostles *and not the one sent* seem to have the steer.

There are those who would argue that scriptural warrant in such processes have no relevance in the context of the contemporary church. Willimon (1988) comments on how Luke appeals to the power of tradition when making decisions. He remarks:

we do know that time and again the Church has attempted to keep itself on track by looking back and letting itself be judged by tradition. Today's Church may not be so convinced of the necessity for contemporary practice conforming to traditional norms. Why should we submit to judgement of the Creed, the scrutiny of scripture, the opinions of the dead? Many are suspicious of the past, seeing it as a repository of misunderstanding, injustice, and benighted ideas.

How the Cuddesdon Twelve make decisions

In their responses to a questionnaire and in a semi-structured interview the Cuddesdon Twelve offer insights into how those at the beginnings of their ministry set about making decisions. We may ask ourselves if our own decision-making process corresponds and consider whether or not it has changed over the years.

A key question was: Did they approach the curacy decision in the same way that they make most decisions or quite differently and, if so, could they say how or why? Respondents were evenly split between those who said they approached this decision in exactly the same way as they approached other decisions and those who regarded this decision as requiring a special or different approach. Among those who declared that they approached a decision about a curacy differently from other major decisions there was a range of responses. They cited the role of prayer in the decision-making process: some being conscious that discernment and decision making on something as explicitly vocational required a more prayerful approach. For example: 'differently from say buying a car or deciding where to holiday, but similar to discerning vocation or choosing a theological college, i. e. with prayer and careful consideration, talking to trusted friends and listening for God.' Most respondents attested, however, to a prayerful approach to the general ordering of their life even if some decisions didn't include explicit prayer. There was a sense, in some respondents, that they were happy that the decision was not entirely within their control and there was an implicit trust in God and in the judgement of other stakeholders.

Respondents decision-making methodology

Each of the 12 respondents was asked about their decision-making style using a planning methodology designed by Etzioni (1989). The key styles he identifies as incrementalism, rationalism and humble decision making were paraphrased in the following form:

Q. 'Which of these three styles of decision making do you think is most like you?

1. I tend to muddle through, making decisions as I need to do so with no long-term plan or vision in mind (Incrementalism).
2. I gather as much data – facts figures and opinions – as I can, and I need to see the 'big picture' before making a decision (Rationalism).
3. I have something of a vision or a plan in mind, and I make a series of decisions designed to help me reach my goal (Humble decision making).

It should be emphasized that the respondents were not told of the category titles used by Etzioni because there was a danger that modest respondents would not have described themselves as 'humble' and would have settled for another option. Here we find an example of the secular and religious use of language: a theme we shall return to in Chapter 8. The 12 respondents included four incrementalists, two rationalists and six humble decision makers.

A respondent who had chosen option one added that he sensed that he had become more like option three as he had matured. Another incrementalist respondent sensed that she had been conditioned into that style by years of serving in the armed forces where there had been an expectation of obedience without asking too many questions about where the action fitted into a grand strategy.

One rationalist respondent described how he spent two weeks researching the proposed curacy benefice and incumbent, learning much from church notices and website, but he admitted that he would have accepted the curacy offer on less information, partly because he thought it unlikely that he would be offered an alternative in his sponsoring diocese, the offer having come with a strong directive from the bishop: 'You are right for Plushton.' Given that directive, his rationale for researching the post so thoroughly was mostly about 'fleshing out' a vision for his prospective ministry there.

For the most part, the six respondents who identified themselves as humble decision makers described a vision that was realistic. They had a clear idea of the decisions (great and small) that needed to be taken to realize the vision. These respondents were keen to emphasize that in their decision-making strategy they were 'buying into' the vision of the Church, the benefice or the prospective incumbent, and that key decisions are corporate as well as individual. This accords well with Etzioni's planning methodology.

How the decision-making process changes when an ordinand is 'released' to seek a curacy in another diocese

The Principal of Ripon College Cuddesdon related how he receives details of curacy vacancies from dioceses around the country. Ordinands still seeking a curacy turn to him for help and respondents attested to the value of his advice throughout the process. The Principal encourages released ordinands to read incoming profiles and, if any resonate, then to discuss the curacy with him. Therein lies the subtle change in the decision-making process: an element of choice from a limited number of options is introduced. The ordinand may browse several curacy profiles *at the same time*, creating an 'options' dimension to the process but, in practice, still may only pursue one at a time.

Identification with the organization

When one contemplates working for an organization one is likely to be interviewed by the prospective employer. It is thought to be good practice to include in the interview process the person(s) with whom one will be expected to work, and to be shown the environment in which one will work. An interview is a two-way process. We ask questions and we try to sense or gauge what it would be like to work in the environment and with the people to whom we are introduced. This also features in a ministerial transition. The Cuddesdon Twelve described what was important to them in a prospective curacy: what they looked for in meetings with the prospective training incumbent, and with other key members of the local church. They had opinions, too, on dioceses which they regarded as having a 'style' or a 'personality' or a churchmanship or gender bias.

All the respondents rated highly the need for a good relationship with the training incumbent. They were asked to rate the importance, to them, of the liturgical style or tradition of the church(es) in their prospective training benefice. Here, the responses ranged considerably. Some ordinands commented that they believed themselves to be quite flexible on such matters: citing their experience at RCC as having brought them to a breadth of understanding or commenting that they thought it might be useful to go to a benefice where the style was relatively unfamiliar to them. For the purpose of this reflection, I have taken together these two considerations: curate/incumbent relationship and liturgical style, because the post-questionnaire interviews revealed some intriguing correlations.

I was alerted to the interconnection between these considerations by an ordinand who described how he had been so 'bowled over' by a prospective incumbent's vision for the mission and ministry of the benefice that he didn't even ask what happens on Sundays. He trusted that if he could identify so well with her vision all else would flow from that, including the worship.

It became clear that, for many respondents, the incumbent iconified the liturgical style. For example, if the incumbent was planning to change liturgical practice (perhaps to lead the congregation towards or away from a eucharistic emphasis) and if the ordinand was similarly inclined, then a rapport was possible. Closer questioning revealed, in many respondents, a need to be able to identify with the theology of the incumbent and hence the liturgical expression of that theology. Fascinating too, was the correlation between the leadership style that was embedded in the theology of the incumbent and was given expression both in the liturgy and in the benefice as a whole.

So, although it didn't matter, too much, to a few respondents, that the liturgical style of a benefice was different from their own, it did matter to them if the prospective incumbent's liturgical, theological and leadership style was different from their own. Ministerial style, they were discovering, was based in a theological perspective and expressed in liturgical style. It seems that incumbents accept an appointment to a benefice, either because the style resonates with them or because they hope to shape the benefice according to their own inclinations. If their theological, liturgical and leadership inclinations accord with those of the curate-to-be, a good working relationship is possible. As one curate put it: 'I liked where he was going, and I want to go with him.'

For a few of the curate respondents hard lessons had been learned. One described how the benefice where he then served was described to him as 'modern catholic'. This had already been a stretch from his 'broad church' background, but he had thought, initially, that the style would be acceptable. When he arrived he became aware that there was a regular service of 'Benediction of the Blessed Sacrament', a practice which greatly challenged his theology of the Eucharist. He raised his concerns with the incumbent who simply insisted that he would be expected, in due course, to lead that service. This became one of many challenges that were not so much about the liturgical practices as about the theology and the leadership style that underpinned them. Over the first year of the curacy there could be no celebration of difference as the incumbent sought to impose his will and the incumbent/curate relationship was in danger of breaking down.

The potential for success in the placement of a curate is to be found not only in theological, liturgical and leadership style resonance, but in generous respect for difference, a need to understand and to be understood, and an openness to potential value of complementary and diverse expressions of collaborative ministry. Related to this is the importance of realistic and reasonable expectations on the part of both the curate and the incumbent. Could this not be said of all ministerial relationships?

Another strong theme to emerge was the importance of ensuring that the ordinand's family were happy with the prospective curacy. Many respondents paid tribute to the support they had received from their family. They spoke of sacrifices made by others in order that they could respond to their call to ordained ministry, and they wanted to ensure that the curacy would be a life-enhancing experience for them as well as for themselves. For some, this was going to be about suitable housing and schools or the location of the benefice. One respondent had felt strongly called to a curacy in an area of great deprivation and danger, but he felt guilty because he and his wife had taken the decision to send their children to schools outside the parish, where the educational environment would be more conducive to their learning and happiness. It took him a while to recognize that he was doing the most loving thing he could do for them.

It was as a result of this interview that I began to explore the question: Is God interested in every detail of every decision we make? Was God interested in which socks I chose to put on this morning or is God only interested in the major decisions? How then does God influence them? Clearly, God has given human beings the ability, for the most part, to make rational decisions but with continual reference back to God for guidance. Comparisons between decision-making processes in the Church and in secular authorities highlights a concern that God might be thought to be less involved or less interested in secular organizational decision making. Some of the authorities in effective decision making are advisers to governments and heads of state. They have helped to guide world leaders through complex problem solving, through the resolution of conflict and in the pursuit of peace between nations. Isn't that a God-given gift applied in a godly way? There would appear to be nothing inherently wrong with secular decision-making theory: it is not a 'Church versus the rest of the world' dichotomy. Perhaps the real issue is not in the process but in the motives and intentions of the decision maker.

Is it not fair to say that some decision making can be complex and fraught with difficulties? If so, then we can do with all the help we can get. We work through a decision with what we have. We may be feeling our way through a very thick fog, unable to see too far ahead and quickly losing sight of whence we came! In this sense the deacon manqué is no less dependent than are any who make a transition in ministry. All are 'deacon'. Croft (1999, p. 53) understands the etymology of 'deacon' as being 'one who comes through the dust'. As we come through the blinding and confusing dust of a ministerial transition we recognize the need to trust God and the decision-making frameworks he sends to guide us. The complexity and contextuality of decision making is explored further in the next chapter.

4

How Climate and Context Affect Discerned Decision Making

Now that we have considered how we make decisions we turn our attention to the climate and context in which we approach a discerned decision about a transition in ministry.

Walking alone

A discerned decision begins, for many, with an idea, a sense, a thought that won't go away. Initially, it may defy articulation, even to oneself. One is alone with it, wrestling with it, walking with it like Kipling's *The Cat That Walked by Himself*. This could be our own story or that of those we have met. Michael's story may serve our reflections.

Michael's story

Michael had completed a postgraduate degree course and was considering his career options. His studies had equipped him for a career in computer technology but he felt uninspired by the prospect. He had always given himself wholeheartedly to everything he had undertaken, so he knew that whatever he did there would be no room for compromise. Michael had become a Christian in his first year at university. He recalled how he was moved by Isaac Watts' great hymn: 'When I survey the wondrous cross'. It was the singing of the final verse that had been the turning point in his faith journey:

Were the whole realm of nature mine,
That were an offering far too small;
Love so amazing, so divine,
Demands my soul, my life, my all.

Michael knew, in his heart, that whatever he did with his life it would be out of his love for God and it would demand his total commitment.

Having made a retreat at a Benedictine monastery, Michael wondered if he might be called to religious life. For a number of reasons he kept this thought to himself. He did so, initially, because he could hardly imagine himself articulating the idea to anyone else. It sounded bizarre, archaic. What would people say? What would his parents think? This was the main reason he said nothing to anyone. His parents had an implicit faith in a divine and overarching being, but they deeply distrusted the institutional Church. Also, Michael was their only child and they longed for grandchildren. How could Michael shatter their dreams? For two years Michael journeyed alone with his growing aspiration. On the pretext of needing 'a bit of space' Michael returned, several times, to the abbey where he had made his retreat. There he would sink happily into the rhythm of worship, study and manual work.

The abbey was set in open countryside and so, whenever possible, Michael would take long walks. He remarked how the distance he could walk and the quality of his experience depended upon many factors: the terrain beneath his feet, the direction of the wind and his mood. Walking with the wind behind him over flat terrain and in high spirits he could walk a very long way before needing rest or refreshment. Michael lamented that rarely were all the optimum conditions met. I asked him if he preferred company on his walks or whether he preferred to walk alone. He replied that it depended on what was on his mind. He mused that, ideally, he would like company to appear and disappear as he journeyed, so that he could think through a problem alone but then share his thoughts from time to time so that, by the end of his journey, he would come to his own conclusion.

Michael's story brings together both the dynamism of life as an ongoing journey and the importance of the climate and context in which we travel while making our decisions. He was wistful for an ideal scenario in which to resolve a problem, to reach a conclusion. He knew, as well as we do, that rarely are the conditions or circumstances of our deliberations entirely conducive, but Michael's wistfulness can give us clues as to what, when it comes to making a discerned decision, might be helpful and what might not. We may ask ourselves if we prefer company in our deliberations or perhaps, like Michael, we prefer to do some deliberating alone, in the knowledge that there are people to whom we can turn, from time to time, people with whom we can share our current thinking.

Are we ever truly alone in our deliberations?

In human terms the answer is 'yes', but the Lord knows our inmost thoughts and meets us in the aloneness of them. We put them away and try to forget about them. The Lord holds them for us and, from time to time, he offers them for further consideration. He is endlessly patient with us. There are times, too, when the thought is right but the timing is wrong. We sense which way our journey should take us but we find the path blocked. This has been the experience of women called to priesthood but whose pathway has been blocked by the institutional Church. And so it was that in the 1990s we saw the emergence of women priests, many of whom had faithfully ministered as deacons or in a lay capacity. Now they could embrace their call and be embraced in the full expression of it: the pathway cleared to the fulfilment of their destiny.

Janice, a lay reader for more than 20 years had shared with her incumbent, many years ago, her deepest thoughts about the possibility of ordained ministry. At that time and in the context of her family circumstances, there was no practical pathway to ordination training. She took the absence of such a pathway as sign that it was not God's will for her. Circumstances have changed and the Church has changed. New and imaginative pathways to training are opening up. Janice has kept abreast of change and has worked and studied faithfully all these years. She has reached a kind of saturation point. She can do no more yet she still feels unfulfilled. A combination of work, home and Church-related changes have caused a shift in the terrain, and she begins to see a pathway that could lead, after all, to ordination.

When restoring the Lost Gardens of Heligan, the restorers discovered that the pathways through the gardens had originally been established over a layer of salt. As a result, weeds and grass had not been able to root too deeply, making it possible to recover the pathways without too much difficulty. This recalled the Lord's question about salt: 'Salt is good; but if salt has lost its taste, how can its saltiness be restored?' (Luke 14.34). If a pathway to ministry was once lost beneath the weeds and grass of circumstance it can be recovered because the 'salt' of the calling has not lost its 'saltiness'.

There are occasions when we might feel we cannot share our inmost thoughts or dilemmas: the nature of the problem or the fear of burdening another can be among the reasons for travelling alone with our decision making. Here we may employ 'ghosts': people from the past who may no longer be available to us. We ask ourselves how they might have received and heard our dilemma, how they might have advised us. Grandparents, parents, siblings, friends, colleagues are, in our imagination, sought out, tried out with deep thoughts currently carried in isolation. Like Michael's ideal scenario, such people can 'appear and disappear' at will.

Occasionally, while wrestling with indecision, a stranger says something that breaks open the cage which constrains our decision making. It might be the woman at the newsagents who brightly comments that there is nothing that cannot be tackled if you have the right tools, or the elderly man who muses that his father taught him to 'plough his own furrow'. These truisms can

be inspirational or they can be infuriating in equal measure, seemingly simplistic philosophies that understate the complexity of the
situation with which we wrestle but, out of their naivety, bring
about change in our thinking.

When asked what it was that changed their perspective on a
problem or how a way forward was formulated, people sometimes remark that it was a brief and unexpected exchange with a
stranger which allowed a major transition to begin. They might
also comment that in such brief exchanges they heard the voice of
God: the stranger being a messenger bringing God's wisdom and
light to a dark place of deliberation.

We read of such encounters in the Bible. Scripture refers to
them as angels, the root word also meaning 'messenger'. There
are occasions, too, when God makes himself present in human
form. The three visitors to Abraham (Genesis 18) is just one
example of such anthropomorphisms. It may not seem right to
seek out such life-changing encounters, but in the midst of deliberation about a major transition in our life journey we do look
for signposts. We don't (yet) have a spiritual satellite navigation
system that tells us in authoritative terms: 'at the next opportunity turn round'. In the midst of our deliberations we have
our 'inside eyes' and our 'inside ears' on high alert for anything
which might inform us or give us the strength and courage to
do that which, deep down, we have already decided is the best
course of action. Sometimes, we need affirmation *before* we act,
as well as after we have acted. Our spoken or unspoken questions, whether to a trusted family member, to a friend or to the
cross on the bedroom wall are: 'Is this the right thing to do?' and
'Was I right to have done this?' These questions are like paren-
theses around the phrasing of our life. Such deliberation takes
place in the maelstrom of discerned decision making as we listen
for the voice of God in the storm (1 Kings 19.11b–13). Michael
referred to the effect on his journey of the terrain beneath his
feet and the direction of the wind. The 'climate' of our decision making can be crucial to our ability to progress. We can be
so easily whipped off our feet by 'every wind of new teaching'
(Ephesians 4.14).

Letting the past inform the present

I suggest that one technique we all employ, from time to time, is that of looking to the past for clues as to how to wrestle with the present or to plan for the future. We look back to the climate in which we made other life-changing decisions. Were we spontaneous or considered in our approach? Did we procrastinate? Did we make lists of pros and cons? We have considered these techniques in a former chapter. Here we consider the *climate* of past decisions and ask ourselves how that climate compares to the present one.

Carol's story

Carol recalled how she felt when she was considering offering herself for ordained ministry. She was restless, excited, fearful, determined and reluctant, all at the same time. She brought all these feelings to the scrutiny of those who were appointed to assess her suitability for ministerial training. Her candour, as well as her many others qualities, served her well. Now, having completed her training, she is considering an offer of a curacy. When asked how she felt about the prospective curacy post, she replied: 'restless, fearful, reluctant'. Gone were the words 'excited' and 'determined'. She had not noticed that her vocabulary was markedly different on this occasion. This led to a discussion in which it became clear that, although the curacy offer had much to recommend it, there was an absence of enthusiasm for it. Carol felt guilty about this, accusing herself of ingratitude towards her sponsoring diocese, but further discussion revealed that Carol could find no spark in the offer which would ignite her, bring the best out of her or employ her gifts. Comparing the climate of her decision making now with that of previous significant transitions Carol was able to begin to articulate why she had significant reservations about her current opportunity. It later transpired that, equipped with a language to explain her reservations, efforts were made by others involved in her appointment more fully to inform her of the context in which she would continue her learning and exercise her ministry. Excitement and determination returned and she was able to accept the offer and, subsequently, found it to be both exciting and life-giving.

It is true that no two situations can be the same. Swinton and Mowat (2006, p. 43) suggest that ideographic knowledge presumes that meaningful knowledge can be discovered in unique, non-replicable experiences. 'It is not possible to step in the same river twice.' The climate and conditions can never be exactly replicated but may offer clues to commonalities that affect the progress of our life. As we work towards a discerned decision our reflections include sample-taking from an ever-rolling river of theological, spiritual and formational experience.

Discerned decision making in a community context

Each of us will make our discerned decisions in a unique combination of contextual and climatic circumstances: the relationship between aloneness in decision making and community discernment depends on many factors. Some of these factors will be beyond our control, others managed by us in ways we have already considered. Here we consider that we rarely make a decision in a unitary community context. We dwell in a multiplicity of communities and each has a different perspective on who we are, depending on the role we play in that community. Who we are influences how we behave. From the 'hub' community of our own home we abide in the communities of our extended family, our friends, our local church, our leisure interests or our employment. We may belong to a virtual community through an internet social network or interest group. As spouse, parent, congregant, teacher, school governor, birdwatcher or martial arts expert, we are cast in roles and speak the language of the context.

Those in community with us have an image of us that may not be cognizant of *all* that we are. If and when we share our deepest aspirations with confidantes from within a multiplicity of community identities we are likely to get a range of opinions based not just on their personal opinion but on who they think we are. We will have shared our aspirations and our story in a multiplicity of community contexts. We may have been reassured because people who know us in different community contexts have, independently, affirmed us in our proposed transition. If we have received different reactions in different community contexts we will have had to work out which opinions in which community contexts are important to us. Does it matter if the friends in the martial arts centre said they just could not see us in a certain role? It might!

Those who are trained for ministry through a largely non-residential course remain members, to some extent, of the communities to which they belonged before they began training. Those in residential training, however, have not left, entirely, the communities from which they came. It is true that the pressure of study and formational activity may mean there is not much time for hobbies or social events. Even the time available for the immediate family is pared away. Those retaining secular employment commitments know that the demands of training can leave little time for anything else (including rest and sleep), therefore, some community associations may be lost. In either setting the ordinand can feel somewhat bereft of certain community associations. The experience of loss may not be immediately obvious nor acute. Undertaking ministerial formation and training entails bereavement: the grief of loss. It has its place alongside feelings of joy and fulfilment with hope and expectation for the future.

Ordinands are in a formational and life-changing transition and for those who remain in secular employment there is an added dimension. They are making that transition in a public arena. Colleagues notice and comment on how they are changing. They may notice changes in language or in reasoning or behaviour. The ordinand observes how their perspective on their workplace changes as they learn to reflect theologically on daily life and events. Ordinands in secular employment are members of a community where colleagues may bring to bear their own cultural context and may express their own views on the ordinand's chosen path. They remember colleagues who affirmed their sense of call. Others, on hearing their intention to be ordained, had begun, immediately, to treat them differently: seeking them out for counsel or comfort, or avoiding them at the coffee machine or avoiding them altogether. Many of those training for ministry non-residentially experience the community of their training course simultaneously with the community of secular employment: an experience which can be hugely challenging yet life-giving.

Discerned decision making in a residential community context

A seminary, is a discrete, distinct and defined community: a microcosm both of a society of individuals with broadly the same goals, and a study in communal Christian living where people worship, eat, study, argue and play together. A closer study of it may further our reflections on the climate and context in which we make a discerned decision about a transition in ministry.

Each year approximately half of the 70 resident ordinands at RCC will leave to take up a curacy post. It is possible to glimpse something of the impact of having 50 per cent of the ordinand community making plans for leaving. This presents a picture of a community in transition. We are beholding a distinct situation in ministerial transition: that is, a significant number of people in transition, together and yet separate.

The new academic year begins in the autumn. First-year ordinands are settling in. The workload is heavy. Those with families are concerned about how children are settling in to new schools and those who have left spouse, children or dependent parents behind are concerned about how their family members are coping without them. Mature adults are living in one small room on a corridor. They are living cheek by jowl with less mature people, creating some critical parent/adolescent behaviours and responses. The regimen of worship and meal times is controlled by the tolling of a bell. They find themselves in quasi-monastic surroundings with a heavy workload and with preoccupations about the places and people they have left behind, and the people and strange surroundings they are now assimilating.

It is with questions in their minds about how the future might look that they listen to the stories told by final year ordinands about the negotiations that are taking place about a curacy. They hear of this insensitive bishop or that unhelpful diocesan officer. They are reassured by those who seem to have 'fallen on their feet' and have secured the curacy of their dreams. So, for some, the climate of decision making has already been coloured as early as the first term of their first year simply by the general level of conversation on the subject. Several respondents remarked that they had been influenced by both the positive and the negative experiences of friends they had made in the year 'above' them. Meanwhile, those in their final year are getting used to the change in the college dynamic caused by the turnover in ordinands. Some are still grieving the loss of friends whom they have followed, over the summer, to distant cathedrals to witness their ordination. They return with heightened awareness that they are in the next tranche of ordinands to fly the nest.

A summer placement has whetted the appetite for ministry or raised more questions than answers. There are reports and essays to write. There may have been 'slippage' due to health or family reasons. It is time to catch up. Most final year ordinands make a great effort to help new ordinands to settle in during the Michaelmas term, take responsibility for social activities and have an increasing role in leading worship both at college and in Sunday placements at local churches. These are all a vital part of the formation of the ordinand and are embraced alongside the completion of academic and pastoral programmes. In short, ordinands in the Michaelmas term of their final year are busy people and, for many, it is during this term, and alongside all their other concerns, duties and responsibilities that there is a curacy to negotiate. For the most part, ordinands do not complain about the timing of this event, nor about the workload and the stress it places on them and their families. They accept that they are preparing to enter a way of life that will make multiple and diverse demands upon them all.

They are asked to make a practical decision at a time when their received theological and ecclesiological 'wisdom' is being challenged by learning and living in community with people of widely differing experiences. There is a climate of new unknowing and they hope that when they emerge blinking into the ordained ministerial sunlight, their efforts will result in an appropriate curacy. Final-year ordinands with a curacy in prospect are not settled people preparing to settle elsewhere. They stand with their sandals on their feet and with a staff in their hands (Mark 6.8–9). They work, they wait, they wonder.

Pressures from beyond

Some ordinands recall times of stress, often exacerbated by what they describe as poor communication. There are comments about periods of non-communication between ordinands and their sponsoring diocese, but these have to be considered in the light of a stressful college climate where even a short period of silence can seem interminable. However, what might seem too trivial to communicate at diocesan level can be of enormous importance to the ordinand. Accounts of 'good practice' include regular contact with the ordinand by the Director of Ordinands, a key figure in the process and one who has accompanied them since the beginning of their journey of discernment and training. The other key figure in the process is the prospective training incumbent: the minister who will shepherd their ongoing learning and formation.

Ordinands tend to ascribe a negative connotation to the absence of response to telephone messages or emails. They need regular encouragement to remember that key figures are likely to be extremely busy or that they are trying to have a much needed 'rest' day, that they may be unwell or away on holiday. Some cope better than others with uncertainty and protracted negotiations. Some ordinands suspect that what they believe to be organizational or communicational inefficiencies are 'dressed up' as protracted pious reflections. One ordinand, for example, related how a prospective incumbent had kept her waiting six weeks before declaring that he did not think she was 'right' for his parish and explained that he was delayed in his response due to 'waiting on God's word'.

Wider contextuality

The climate for discerned decision making at a crucial stage of emergence from training to deployment is also characterized by broader ecclesial issues. These include financial constraint, the search for, and the training of suitable incumbents to shepherd the newly ordained ministerial lamb. There are also issues relating to the availability of compatible learning environments within the rich diversity of traditions in the Church of England. The barometric reading of the climate of discerned decision making also comprises elements of the unpredictable winds of individual diocesan policies and procedures and the changing environment of the Church as a whole.

Families in transition

Previously we noted that one cannot put one's hand in the same river twice. Let us revisit that metaphor and note that when one puts one's hand in the river, there are ripple effects: the water is disturbed, albeit briefly. We have considered just a few of the 'ripple effects' of articulating a sense of call to a transition in ministry. We have noted how family members are affected by the possibility. What we might consider now is how the ripple effects of those close to the minister can shape the transition.

Theological college, seminary, and non-residential courses are all communities in transition and comprise ordinands with families: vital communities within the community. Here we acknowledge that family members are undertaking their own transition in ministry. Wives and husbands of ordinands speak of their own heartache, their loss of familiar roots and support networks and of the challenges brought about by ministerial training and formation. Although many make heroic adjustments to accommodate their spouse in the pursuit of their vocation, some difficulties are not resolved. As a couple, as a family, they embark on ministry that will be characterized by further transitions and by relocation, bringing to the fore many of the issues experienced in the run up to, and during, training. It can be easy to be carried along by the adventure of ministry in the service of the Lord and to assume that one's wife or husband shares the same vision with all its consequent trials and tribulations (not forgetting all its joys and satisfiers). Mark and Sharon's story may illustrate this point.

Mark and Sharon's story

Mark related how he had a sense of a call to ordained ministry in his late teens but he had tried to ignore it, concentrating instead on his university education and a career in law. The sense of call never left him, and finally he began to articulate it, first to his parish priest and then to his wife, Sharon. The parish priest was encouraging and wanted to make a telephone call, there and then, to the DDO. Sharon, on the other hand, was distraught at the prospect. She knew what a life-changing course was in prospect for them both. Sharon had a career which rooted her, for the foreseeable future, to her current location. She, too, understood her work to be God's will for her. She was angry with God and with Mark for bringing this disruptive idea of ordained ministry into their lives. Mark and Sharon believed that their relationship was God-given, that they had a vocation to be married. Neither could hold that Mark's sense of call to ordained ministry could be authentic if it put such strain on their marriage that they separated. It took love, courage, generosity, patience and honesty in the climate of their discerned decision making to keep their relationship intact. It would be eighteen months before they could both sit down with the DDO to explore the matter further.

'Is it about me, Lord; or is it about them?'

Here we must consider that a transition in ministry may not be appropriate because of some new vision of the minister's, but because another family member's needs, desires, vision or aspirations have priority. Sometimes, if one listens carefully to someone's description of their ministerial journey, one can hear at what point they assumed that their own journey was the only one that mattered. Sadly, some ministers, whose relationships had been destroyed along the way, realize too late how important it is to minister to one's own family as well as to others.

The aspirations of family members bring about transitions of many kinds. Sadly, the pursuit of those aspirations can break up a family unit. Sometimes the aspiration itself is merely an expedient to justify a transition which will bring about a deeply desired separation. Those involved in the process of discernment and assessment regarding aspirants to ordained ministry are aware of this possibility.

Derek and Sally's story

Derek had completed a three-year appointment as a curate. His journey into ministry began in the north of England. He had not wished to return to his sponsoring diocese on completion of his training. Once details of curacy vacancies had been posted in his college, he became excited at the prospect of a curacy in the south of England. Now it was time for Derek to move from his curacy into a post of 'first responsibility'. Derek's ministry had been much praised. His bishop was keen to retain him and encouraged him to look at a benefice just ten miles away from where he and Sally were living. Derek was thrilled. The benefice had much to offer. There was potential for church growth. There were opportunities for 'outreach', the style of the church was one with which he was comfortable and the rest of the ministry team were congenial, committed and enthusiastic.

Following Derek and Sally's visit to the prospective benefice, they talked together late into the night about the potential of ministry in that place. They talked about the benefice house and garden. In their mind's eye they had the furniture moved in (yes, the three-seater settee would fit in the living room), and they had the pictures hung on the walls. As days went by, however, Sally became more and more pensive. At first, Derek did not notice. He was flying high on the prospect of 'his own patch' and the freedom to shape and exercise his ministry. It was during one such flight of fancy that Sally dropped her coffee mug on the stone floor of the curacy house kitchen. It brought them both, quite literally, down to earth, as they scrambled to sweep up the broken pieces of crockery and to mop up the coffee. Then, very quietly, Sally said: 'Derek, I don't want to go there.' Derek sat back on the floor. He was stunned. Neither of them spoke for a few minutes. Sally broke the silence: 'I don't like it down here in the south. I am a northern girl, and I feel like an alien. I thought I would get used to it but I can't. I'm sorry, Derek.' They both wept silently.

Sally hailed from Manchester. Her elderly and frail parents lived on the Wirral. It was a constant source of worry to Sally that she could not get 'home' very often and could not help her sister who had day-to-day responsibility for their parents. When they were in the North, it was fairly easy to visit, but it had been six years since they left, and her parents had become more dependent. Her sister had twice postponed a hip replacement operation because of the care her parents needed. In addition, she missed the familiarity of her northern roots: the language, the humour, the culture. Sally's needs and those of her family had not been considered as bishop, prospective benefice council members and her husband had become caught up in the excitement of the proposed new post.

For three days, quiet (not gloom) settled on the home of Sally and Derek. They went about their daily chores and commitments. The new job was not mentioned. One evening, while they both sat watching something quite uninspiring on the television, Derek said: 'I'm sorry, Sal. I hadn't thought. I love you very much, and I don't believe in a God who would expect me to neglect the needs of my family for the interests of the institutional Church.' After a few more minutes he went on: 'What I found attractive about the job, the potential for church growth, opportunities for working with people on the edge, and all that. Well, I can do that anywhere. I'm going to turn the job down. It can't be right if it is not right for both of us.'

Six month later, Derek and Sally moved into the vicarage of a parish on the edge of town in the north-west of England. In their Christmas letter to friends they wrote, excitedly, of the welcome they had received, the opportunities there and the vision they shared for ministry in that place.

Not forgetting the children

The aspirant to ministerial transition may have children to consider. When considering children it is not only the uprooting of them from their home and a change of school that is involved (as if that we not momentous enough!), it is also the leaving of friends and familiar haunts and the possibility of verbal abuse and bullying just because one of their parents is a 'vicar'. Christian ministry is sacrificial ministry, but the sacrifices of those who support or surround the minister cannot be overestimated, and they cannot be expected or taken for granted.

Daring to listen to God in the voices of others

There are so many reasons (not all of them bad) why the minister in transition can become the centre of their own universe. Part of discerning a call is making the effort to see an idea from the perspective of the lives of all those who will be affected by the pursuit of it. Some people are wary of this. They fear that such empathetic deliberation will be a distraction from hearing God's voice. I suggest that, on the contrary, the authenticity of a call is more likely to be discerned among the perspectives of other stakeholders in our lives. The most powerful voices, however, may not be the ones to heed. A collection of small voices can drown out the powerful voice. The Spirit of God can speak softly, gently and over a period of time. Unfortunately, we may have a higher regard for the spectacular phenomena than we do for the gentle prompting of the Spirit that comes to us through the many voices of family, friends, colleagues, advisers and strangers. I recall a candidate for ministry who was not recommended for training by the Bishops' Advisory Panel. There were a number of issues, but there was a comment in the report that the candidate had told no one in the parish of their intention to seek support for training for ordained ministry. All their references were extra-parochial (there being no incumbent of the parish at that time). No one who knew them well was able to pray, affirm or to gently offer reservations. There was little or no contextual discernment of their vocation.

The effect of church culture on discernment

Before we leave the contextual and climatic aspect of transitions in ministry we may want to consider church culture and conditioning. It may be that our nurture in Christian discipleship has conditioned us to accept, unquestioningly, the decisions of others. The bishop says go, so you go! One ordinand, wrestling with indecision about a curacy offer, longed for the decision to be taken away from him. Exasperated, he asked: 'Why can't we be given our "marching orders" on the last day of our training?' Clearly, this is an option and one which is employed in some parts of the universal Church. Whether or not that approach makes the best use of ministerial resources is a matter for debate and beyond the scope of this book. What might be of interest is that the ordinand in question was unmarried and had a military service background.

In summary, a discerned decision about a transition in ministry has to be made contextually: taking into account the needs of others including family members and the wider church. Decisions are affected by the perspective others bring to our deliberations and it can be hard to discern the voice of God from within the cacophony of the voices of those who are stakeholders in the decision and those who merely express an opinion and have no axe to grind. Although it is easy to place ourselves at the centre of deliberations about a transition in ministry, it may be the transitional needs of another which affects our own transition.

It would be a mistake to assume that all climactic or contextual factors are a hazard, an inconvenience or a challenge. Many factors highlight the importance of discerning in community: both the community which nurtures the idea of a transition in ministry and the community which will be most affected by the consequences of the discerned decision. Nurture and formation rarely take place in isolation: not least is nurture and formation within the community and unity of the Holy Trinity.

Connectedness to God should not be understood as disconnectedness from the world around us. We seek and find God in the world wherein we are engaged and we serve God in serving the world. Discerned decisions are made where we live and we live in God and in the world. Although it may seem that much of our 'wrestling with God' takes place inwardly where we meet and engage with God, our discerned decisions are explored, tried and tested as we engage with God in the world about us.

5

Navigating Through Difficulties

Just as I am, though tossed about
with many a conflict, many a doubt,
fightings and fears within, without,
O Lamb of God, I come.

The reader may recognize this verse from the well-known hymn
'Just as I am' written by the English poet Charlotte Elliott
(1789–1871). Some of her close family members were clergy in
the Church of England so perhaps she recognized something of
their inner turmoil as well as her own. She was an invalid and
no stranger to suffering. Dr John Julian (1892) wrote of her that
'though week and feeble in body, she possessed a strong imagination and a well-cultured and intellectual mind'. He describes her
verse as 'characterized by tenderness of feeling, plaintive simplic-
ity, deep devotion, and perfect rhythm'. Living with conflict and
doubt while retaining grace and serenity is not easy but it has
been demonstrated inspiringly by many over the centuries.

In this chapter we consider further how we manage a transition
in ministry. Some of the challenges we face are internal turmoil as
we work through an idea of a transition. They are the inner voices
of doubt: the mental wrestling with God that can be a feature of
our deliberations. Other challenges include the managing of expectations and how we come through difficulties that arise from a
mismatch of expectations, how we reconcile differences in vision
or ministerial style. We consider how we move through times of
low motivation or burnout. A time of transition in ministry is a
time of being betwixt and between. We consider how the first
disciples managed such a time in their own ministry.

Managing ourselves in transition

Our personality, rooted somewhere in our nature or our nurture, will affect how we make a transition. Those of us who worry about everything will worry our way through the move. Those of us who are relaxed about everything are likely to be relaxed about a move. Is it too obvious to suggest that we are who we are? Difficulties may arise, however, when we try to compare our coping with that of another. Back come those inner voices telling us we ought to be better organized or that we shouldn't have let a certain difficulty trouble us. We considered in the previous chapter the way our transitions affect other people. In this sense our natural inclination to be a worrier may mean we hassle those who are trying their best to help us to a successful outcome. Those of us who are very relaxed may frustrate those who need answers or actions from us. In addition, what we consider to be obstacles or difficulties may appear to others as no problem at all. A dimension of a transition in ministry is, therefore, the way we manage who we are throughout the process: having a care for how our words and actions, our pauses and our inactions, may adversely affect the process and colour the outcome. Our expectations of ourselves, of others and of the ministry in prospect may be unrealistic, creating further difficulties.

By the time we arrive in a new place of ministry we may have lost something of our initial enthusiasm: the vision we had, clouded by dismay and disappointment. The way transitions in ministry work in the Church of England means that there can be several months between the initiation of the process and the arrival in post. A curate remarked that by the time he arrived in his title post it had been 18 months since he had first met his training incumbent. The curate recognized that he, himself, had 'moved along a lot' in that time but he hadn't allowed that the incumbent (and the parish) had also moved along a bit! The curate commented that the ministry he found on arrival was quite different from the ministry he had glimpsed early in the interview stage and which had fed his imagination in the intervening time. I should add that what he found on arrival was more exciting and rewarding than he had been expecting.

Aspirations and expectations

There are many factors that contribute to arrival at a place of reconciliation or acceptance of a ministry. Clearly, if our expectations of a prospective ministry are low we are unlikely to be disappointed; but such a stance would have to be traded off against the buzz of excitement we can feel when we take a risk. A friend of mine was once accused, by a colleague, of being 'a fool floating on a cloud of optimism', but are we not called to be fools for the sake of Christ (1 Cor. 4.10)? My friend has high expectations of himself and of others, but he is not unrealistic: he is not out of touch with the way people are and what one can reasonably expect of oneself or others. There are times when he feels let down by people or he is disappointed in what he has been able to achieve, but he is reconciled to who he is and knows himself well enough (likes himself enough?) to accept himself and a situation for what it is.

The Cuddesdon Twelve were asked what they saw ahead of them: what they hoped for and what they expected to find the other side of the ordination service. They reported that during their training their vision appeared to change at each turn of the process. How they articulated their vision changed too, as their 'God-speak' vocabulary enlarged. They reported how they had grown in knowledge and confidence and in their ability to express the almost inexpressible: the nature of what it is that they believe God is calling them to be, to do and to become. Their insight into what ordained ministry is about had changed through their experience of formal education and through their parish placements. One ordinand declared that even until arriving at college he had little knowledge of what his parish priest did between Monday and Saturday! They demonstrated increasing awareness of what they were and the awesomeness of what they were offering to God and his Church.

Some respondents spoke of personal sacrifice. They aspired to going where they were sent, and to doing what needed to be done. They spoke of willingly giving up a permanent home or giving up the prospect of earning a high income. They expected to be challenged at every level. They said that they had found their time in training to be life-changing, their theological and ecclesiological preconceptions thrown into the air. They reported times when they were unclear about what they believed, their views changing by the week. Some had not expected such an upheaval in their belief-base and some had come to realize how little they knew of the Church of England, let alone the Anglican Communion. One respondent declared that he did not expect to discover how little he knew about practically everything!

I asked the Cuddesdon Twelve what they wanted from the stakeholders: those who would deploy them and those who would supervise their ongoing learning and formation. They said they expected to be treated like adults, and as people who have given up much to follow their Lord. This has not sounded like: 'The Church should be grateful I offered myself for ordained ministry', but there was an expectation that they and their family would be treated with some respect.

When discussing housing, for example, some ordinands described how a diocese had been keen to offer a curacy, but had no suitable accommodation to offer. This had been given, by two respondents, as the sole reason why they had rejected a curacy offer, as it 'sent out a mixed message' regarding welcome and caring. Single ordinands had expressed their dismay at being offered inadequate accommodation, since they were alone and 'wouldn't need much space'. For the most part, single ordinands, or married ordinands with no children, expected to be treated equitably in comparison to married ordinands with children. Respondents ranked housing as the third most important consideration after the incumbent/curate relationship and the compatibility of church tradition, theology and teaching.

It would be a mistake to leave an impression that the aspirations and expectation of the Cuddesdon Twelve resided solely or largely in the area of 'pay and rations'. They expressed, in one way or another, their aspirations for service in the building of the Kingdom of God. The problem was that when they first met with diocesan stakeholders to discuss a curacy idea they assumed everyone concerned knew of their high motivation, but what was foremost in their minds, alongside collegial relational concerns, were basic needs for provision for themselves and their family.

It is not within the scope of this book to judge if expectations are unreasonable, though a few respondents asked that question of me. Some of them had unreasonable expectations of themselves. For some, their academic grades will never be good enough, their personal spiritual disciplines wanting and their zeal all-consuming. With help and support, most had come to a degree of self-awareness and to an acceptance of themselves before God, often with endearing and self-deprecating humour. Overwhelmingly their priorities were to serve God and to grow in their ministry but this did not negate the expectation that their basic needs would be met.

Far outweighing accounts of unhelpfulness or insensitivity are accounts of how hard people work to discern the will of God in placing a curate, in finding a suitable and compatible training incumbent and in securing good quality housing in a suitable location. For the most part loving, prayerful and generous attentiveness characterize the process. Some of the Cuddesdon Twelve saw the outworking of this attentiveness during the process while others only saw it in hindsight. Regrettably, people are more likely to share accounts of when things had gone wrong than they are to share accounts of things having worked out well.

There is a deep desire among all the stakeholders to 'get it right' more often and so reduce the incidence of 'curacy breakdown' with all the consequential pain and expense. The deep commitment of stakeholders to the best possible outcome is both obvious and understated, which may account for why some ordinands, themselves likely to be hypersensitive at a crucial time of transition, may not always form an objective view of a situation.

David Runcorn (in Witcombe 2005, p. 97) states that the Church is committed to the nurture, development and training of the newly ordained. He says it is an area that has received 'a considerable amount of professional planning and resourcing'. Also, a particular diocese will have 'its own vision, priorities and strategy for ministry'. Nevertheless, many respondents were baffled by diocesan procedural variations.

Six of the Cuddesdon Twelve, reporting on how they came to a decision about a curacy, commented on differences between what they had expected the curacy to be like and how it had turned out. There was no common experience, no commonality of correlation between expectation and outcome. Comments ranged from 'much as I had expected' to 'more than I could have hoped for'. None regretted being ordained but one regretted the choice of curacy. After a long struggle for both him and his training incumbent the curate was relocated and is now thriving, experiencing much of his anticipated delight in ministry.

Statistically, he demonstrates what the Principal of RCC reported as the 'one in ten' curacies that 'break down'. Having had deep discussions with the curate concerned, there would seem to be no sign that his expectations of ordained ministry were unrealistic. He is mature and worldly wise and his vision and zeal is inspiring. Would we want any less from those entering ordained ministry? Those early years in ministry can be challenging and so much depends on the curate/training incumbent relationship. We noted, previously, that the incumbent/curate relationship is crucial to the successful outcome of the curacy, far outstripping any other considerations of family or accommodation. A significant dimension of that relationship is the implicit and explicit negotiation and agreement of expectations, both those of the newly arriving minister and those of the people who will receive them.

Those in curacies felt that there was little room for negotiation. They recognized that they did not know what, in ministerial terms, is negotiable, and there was a sense, in most instances, that the training incumbent held tightly to the reins of authority, certainly at the beginning of the curacy. Some curates thought this unreasonable. Subsequently several curate respondents said they had come to recognize the wisdom of the training incumbent in offering structure and discipline in the first year or two.

Mismatches

When mismatches between curate and benefice or incumbent occur, the anecdotal evidence suggests that there can be significant distress and strained relationships not only between ministerial colleagues within the benefice but within the curate's household. Arguably, in such circumstances, the quality of the experience is likely to be impaired. In some instances relocation becomes necessary, with all the consequent upheaval and additional expense to both the church and the curate. It is the stated aim of the Church at both national and diocesan level to reduce the incidence of mismatch resulting in relocation of the curate. Considerable effort and resources are being poured into the selection, training and support of training incumbents as well as into careful and prayerful consideration of the placing of curates. Church authorities recognize that, at a time of financial constraint, it is more important than ever that the Church make best use of its ministerial resources so that we may more effectively proclaim the gospel and so fulfil our corporate calling. Helping ministers to fulfil their own sense of call within that includes helping and supporting ministers at every transition in ministry.

The Principal: an honest broker

During the months preceding ordination the Principal of RCC offers himself as an 'honest broker', helping approximately 120 residential and non-residential ordinands each year to find a suitable curacy. He remarks, however, that some ordinands, particularly those retained by their sponsoring diocese, need little or no assistance from him. The Principal works, reportedly, on 'the 80:20 principle': 80 per cent of the ordinands generate approximately 20 per cent of his workload in respect of his brokering role, whereas 20 per cent of ordinands generate approximately 80 per cent of the work. His task includes probing what is being expected of the ordinand and what the ordinand is expecting of the curacy, those with the greatest need for help being those with unrealistic expectations. He might ask: 'Is it going to be a dangerous place for the ordinand?' By this he asks if there are signs of potential incompatibility between the proposed training incumbent and the curate-to-be. There may, for example, be a lack of sympathy with aspects of the curate's personal, social, or marital arrangements. Disclosures on the part of the prospective incumbent have been known to 'ring alarm bells' that have led the Principal to recommend to the ordinand that they 'look elsewhere', or to the receiving diocesan authorities that they reconsider where to place the ordinand. Such interventions attest to the level of concern for all involved and a desire to maximize the likelihood of a successful curacy appointment. He commented that, in addition to the one-in-ten situations where the curacy breaks down, a further one-in-ten curates will experience significant difficulties with related stress and unhappiness. Stakeholders recognize that, in addition to their own knowledge and experience of candidates for ordination, some of whom have been treading the pathway to ordination for a considerable amount of time, those with recent experience of the ordinand, experience gained during training, have valuable insights to offer in regard to ability, disposition and behaviour. The Principal is in a position to challenge ordinands, to encourage them to consider curacy vacancies that they might otherwise overlook. Andrew's story may serve to illustrate this point.

Andrew's story

Andrew, who had been told from the outset that he would be released from his sponsoring diocese, looked to the Principal for vacant curacy posts. The Principal asked him if he minded where he went. He replied that he did not. The Principal selected one curacy profile document from among many that had arrived from dioceses around the country and encouraged Andrew to consider it. When he read the details, Andrew 'laughed out loud', as the training benefice was the opposite of anything he might have chosen. He threw the profile document away but, following two days of reflection and prayer, he had to retrieve it from the municipal recycling bin to give the idea more consideration. He explored the post and subsequently accepted it. He settled very happily into his title post and still believes that 'God is in the system'. Andrew has always loved a challenge. He is wise and mature with a wealth of experience of the wider Church, and one senses that the Principal recognized this when suggesting the post to him.

Once a connection is made between the ordinand and the appropriate diocesan officer the remainder of the process is, systemically and reportedly, the same as for those ordinands who were retained, but things do not always go smoothly. Problems can arise and many respondents gave examples. These included new reservations about the curacy, either in the mind of the ordinand or in the mind of the Principal, arising either after negotiations had begun or even after an agreement had been reached. There may be problems regarding suitable housing or schooling, or issues about ongoing formal education and the completion of degree programmes.

For the most part, the newly ordained set about their ministry with energy and enthusiasm. Some will say that nothing had quite prepared them for the volume of work they would undertake or the pressures they would experience.

Burnout

Sadly, some ministers will become overwhelmed and exhausted, physically, emotionally and spiritually. Some will experience the state that is termed 'burnout'. In the Introduction to his book on ministry burnout Sanford (1982) describes the state of burnout as 'a person who has become exhausted with his or her profession or major life activity'. He goes on to describe how this affects a person physically, emotionally and spiritually. His helpful book includes a chapter on 'dealing with expectations'. Sanford says: 'as we have seen, the ministering person is faced with so many different expectations that they can never be satisfied. He can wear himself out trying to satisfy these expectations, or exhaust himself in anxiety because he cannot.' If we have reached that point it can be difficult to consider a move to another kind of ministry or to a similar ministry in a different location: either one of which may be God's way of renewing and revitalizing us. We may be so despondent that we cannot be persuaded, or persuade ourselves, that a move would be a good thing for us and, possibly, for the people we have been serving. We may have lost confidence in God, in the Church or in ourselves. We may have lost sight of our gifts and skills. The measures used to assess our ministry may have led us to believe that we have failed, and so we reason that if we have failed in this place, we would fail anywhere. Sanford (p. 78) suggests some questions we might ask ourselves if we think we are a failure:

> When we contemplate failure we need to ask three questions: Are we failing because of some fault of our own? Are we failing because we are in a situation in which we cannot possibly win? Are we really failing or do we only think we are failing because we are measuring success by the wrong standards?

Those in a state of burnout, those overcome or overwhelmed by expectations, their own or other peoples (real or imagined), need time, patience and skill to be gently restored to the point where they can begin to see the possibility of continuing in their ministry or making a move to a new and, hopefully, life-giving ministerial environment. Diocesan officers, professional counsellors and charitable organizations such as the Society of Martha and Mary do much to help ministers to avoid burnout and to help them through to renewed energy. From a supported position they may be able to consider a life-giving transition in ministry or a life-giving transition out of ordained ministry altogether.

Vocation in time and place

Perhaps this leads us to consider the question: 'Are some vocations temporary?' We may ask in reply: 'Aren't all vocations temporary in the great and eternal scheme of things?' We no longer live in a 'job for life' culture but if we are not doing the same thing in old age as we were doing when we were in our teens, does that mean we got it wrong? Perhaps we can see, rather, that one decision led to another and we came to realize our vocation incrementally. On the other hand, we may have done widely different things in our lifetime, some of which seem unconnected one to another. Are all or any of those things designated by us, or by others, as having been a mistake because they stand out as different or because the experience was an unhappy one? Perhaps we are conditioned to remember or promote those jobs or experiences which went well. How many people, when writing a CV put a value judgement in the margin next to the entry? For example, '1983–1984, Hairdresser's Assistant (wasn't much good at it)'. Reading the subtext of a CV and sharing impressions of what seemed to have been life-giving can help someone to recognize what might be the seed-bed of the next great adventure, even if the idea is being revisited decades after a first attempt at it. Stories abound of women and men who sensed a call to ordained ministry quite early in life but who, because of circumstances or distraction, did not revisit that call until much later in life.

What then of so-called 'bad' experiences? A work or relational experience that had previously been designated a failure may be the source of new growth, new insights or passion for a cause. What we have done in the past and what we have suffered or endured might become the foundation of our ministry and a way in which God is redeeming that earlier experience. Those who assess our suitability for ordained ministry are more interested in how we came through our bad experiences or coped with our failures than the fact that we had such experiences or that we failed in some way. In short, that venture or experience that looked or felt wrong or destructive then might be an important part of our ministry now and in the future.

Transitions as times betwixt and between

By relating to both the positive and negative aspects of a transition in ministry I have tried to relate faithfully to the world view of those who have so generously shared their experience of transition, as well as bringing a flavour of my own experience in this regard. I have done this not just to offer a balanced view but to bring to the subject a sense of the oscillation that we experience as we weigh both the positive and negative aspects of a transition in ministry. Being in transition is being betwixt and between. I am not suggesting that this is a bad thing. Is not our whole life a be-twixt and between experience? Betwixt and between is the reality: it is where we dwell and this can be felt most acutely at times of transition. If we want a New Testament hermeneutic of betwixt and between we may find it useful to reflect on the experience of the first disciples of Jesus during the time between his ascension into heaven and the day of Pentecost.

Transition of the disciples of Jesus: ascension to Pentecost

It was a poignant time for the disciples of Jesus: and not just for the eleven who feature so prominently in the Gospel accounts. All those who had followed Jesus to his death and had witnessed his resurrection had begun to sense that not only was he about to leave them, but that their own lives were going through a major transition. Life was not the same as it had been before the passion of Christ. To some extent, in this in-between time, life might have seemed surreal. Jesus would appear and disappear. He would walk through walls and host a barbecue beach party.

There would be very human questions: 'What does this mean for us? What will be expected of us? How will we cope?' These questions resonate with us at a time of change. Jesus anticipated some of their questions and understood their unspoken anxieties. He reassures them. He becomes reconciled to Peter (and others?) who had deserted him or denied their association with him. He draws Thomas deep into his own wounds to strengthen his faith and that of them all.

Luke's account of the events leading up to the ascension (Luke 24) offers us clues as to how Jesus prepares us for our own transi-tions. In verses 50–53 Luke describes how Jesus 'led them out as far as Bethany' and how he 'blesses' them. We read how Jesus 'withdrew from them' and is carried up into heaven, and how the disciples worshipped him, how they return to Jerusalem with great joy, and are to be found continually in the Temple blessing God.

Let us 'unpack' those phrases, those verses of Scripture which imply so much, and see what they can teach us about coping with being launched into the unknown of a new ministerial venture.

'He led them out as far as Bethany'

Bethany was a special place for Jesus. It was a community within community. It was Jesus' 'cell group', a place of rest and refreshment, a place of fellowship and sharing. The Gospel accounts imply that only a few gathered at the home of Martha, Mary and Lazarus at Bethany, but perhaps there were times when the whole band crowded into the house and needed feeding. Little wonder Martha was 'busy about many things' (Luke 10.40). We may ask ourselves about our own recent 'public' and 'private' ministry. Looking back over the last year, how has Jesus ministered to us in both public and private ways? Where has Bethany been for us? Was it there that the first inkling came that we may be about to begin a period of transition? In whose ministry was the prophetic word or the pastoral observation that we seemed to be entering a state of 'in between'? Who 'anointed' our feet ready for the beginning of a new journey? Did we hear their words or sense their actions as being those of Jesus?

'He blessed them'

During the weeks between the resurrection and the ascension Jesus had been ministering to his disciples. He had appeared and disappeared. He had been present and absent: all of which was bewildering and confusing for the disciples. They had learned to cope with his mystical presence and with his apparent absence, learning to make choices and decisions on how to live and how to survive. It is likely that there were rows and disagreements; arguments about what Jesus had actually said or taught. There would be discussions about what they should do or where they should go next. In that sense the Church has not changed at all! But they had been blessed too: blessed by his presence, by his words and by his promises that he would be always with them. How have we been blessed in recent times and by whom has his blessing come? Amid trials and tribulations and controversy and some of the most disappointing behaviour we have seen among Christian people; how have we been blessed? Perhaps that blessing has included the blessing of departure in words such as 'You really should go for your health's sake, for your sanity's sake', or perhaps, 'For our sake'. Permission to move on can be a real blessing. For some, there may have been disappointments, let downs, hurts, sadnesses, pain and loss. Can we sense how Jesus has ministered to us in such times? Do we sense through whom he has done so?

'He withdrew from them'

When a small child learns to come down a staircase safely, the parent waits for them at the foot of the stairs and tries to judge whether to hold on to some control or to let go and let the child take a risk. The parent has to balance the need for the child to take a risk with providing a safety net to prevent the child from coming to harm. The child, seeing the parent at the foot of the stairs, is apt to launch out into the air, confident that the parent will catch them. Do we ever sense that Jesus has withdrawn from us and do we put a negative connotation on that, or do we interpret it as Jesus letting us take a risk?

This betwixt and between time is a time for holding on and for letting go; but letting go of what? *Holding On and Letting Go* is the title of Chris Leonard's book (2009). On the back cover we read:

> Sometimes it is right to hold on to something, sometimes better to let go. But there is often a creative tension around assessing how to act. And in God's economy, it may be that letting go of old ties makes it possible for God to bless us in new ways.

What are we letting go of at a time of transition? Are we letting go of hurts, disappointments and grudges: letting go of the mistakes we have made and letting go of the times of betrayal, of faithlessness and despondency? A new start affords an opportunity to let go of these things. It may be that we need to let go also of certain attachments, no matter how treasured they have been until now.

It may be time to let go of self-doubt. During this period of transition the disciples had their eyes opened to the power of God in the risen Christ, and they were beginning to glimpse the power with which they would be invested. Perhaps they would be somewhat overawed by such power and extremely conscious of their shortcomings. 'I am not worthy!' I hear people cry when a new and awesome ministry is laid upon them. 'No, you're not!' I reply. 'None of us are. Get over it; hold it, embrace it, in the trust and confidence God places in you to bring his work to good effect.'

Having our eyes opened to God and all he can do through us helps us to capture his vision for the world and our share in the realization of that vision, whether that contribution is to be small or great. Thomas had his vision opened up but so did all the others. We too, must be people of vision if we are to help forward the Kingdom of God. If there are barriers to belief they may well be barriers of prevarication and procrastination. We may be just plain scared and God understands that too, but the truth is that to believe is to respond. There are no bystanders and observers to the building of the Kingdom. Sometimes our vision for the Kingdom in our own locality may be too narrow or too small. Together, and individually, we can only be faithful to Christ and his mission in the world if we dare to have a bigger vision. For some, optimism does not come naturally. Such people will say, of themselves, 'I am a "glass half empty" sort of person.' The size of the task we are given to do and the grace we are given to do it render a 'glass' that is exactly the right size and is full to the brim!

Matthew on the ascension

The emphasis in Matthew's account is not on the ascension itself so much as on Jesus giving authority to his disciples. We might have expected from Matthew some resonance with the Old Testament account of the ascension of Elijah and the 'falling of the mantle' on Elisha (2 Kings 2.13). Although Matthew makes no direct reference to either character here, there is resonance with the passing on of authority to the disciples. It is worth noting, too, that in Matthew, Jesus draws near. He is not taken from them. He does not draw away. Matthew ends not by looking back but by looking forward, to the authorized ministry each apostle would be given.

Jesus is with his disciples throughout this transitional period, bringing counsel, permission to move on, blessing and authority. For their part, the disciples have only to wait to be clothed with power from on high and to accept the authority given them by Jesus and the gifting of the Holy Spirit that would enable them to carry out Christ's mission in the world. Comforted, strengthened, excited but nervous, they spend the waiting time in worship and praise. Surely, therein lies a formula for living in a time of betwixt and between? Sustaining a mood of optimism and joy throughout a transition can be hard but if we can draw on the spiritual disciplines that sustain us when we are not in an explicit transition and sustain them during the transition we may find we survive rather better. Alison's story may illustrate this.

Alison's story

Alison tells of a transition from parish ministry to a diocesan appointment that was fraught with difficulties. Preparing the parishioners for an interregnum proved more difficult than she had expected. Their reluctance to see her go was evidenced in truculent behaviour. There was confusion about a starting date for the new job and considerable negotiation regarding where she was to be based. There were difficulties over housing and problems with removal firms. Alison declared that if she hadn't maintained her pattern of daily prayer she would not have coped. She commented that she would not have arrived in her new post with the energy it would require from the first day if she had not constantly sought the help of God and maintained her sense of humour; a gift for which she thanked God daily.

It had not been easy for Alison to make the move from parish ministry to a role which involved enabling the ministry of others but kept her one step away from the general public. Despite her willingness to serve where she was required she did not find it easy to surrender the immediate satisfaction of her former ministry, but she did not bear this cost in a martyred sort of a way. Her characteristic cheerfulness and optimism, her trust in God and in her diocesan colleagues, carried her through. She came to appreciate that his new role was just as life-giving as her previous role, just as connected to the building of the Kingdom of God. She understood this in terms of the words of Jesus: 'I came that they might have life: life in its fullness' (John 10.10). For her, the fullness of life came in obedience and service to God: in losing her life in order to gain it (Matt. 10.39).

How one perceives and bears the cost of discipleship will depend on many factors. Alison has experienced, and will no doubt continue to experience, hardship, challenge and cost in her discipleship but she does not court it: she does not seek it as if doing 'the hard thing' for God is more laudable than doing something that presents no difficulties. One meets ministers who are not satisfied unless there is hardship or trauma, pain and suffering in their ministry. A religious brother once declared to me: 'If it doesn't hurt, brother, it can't be God's will.' Really?

When considering a transition in ministry it is worth exploring, perhaps with a friend or confidante, whether one feels driven to a possible ministry or whether one feels drawn; whether the prospect of it (costly or not) seems life-giving or life-draining. Does the narrative of the prospective ministry contain the words 'ought', 'should' or 'must'? Perhaps it is God's will one ought, should, must obey; but caution is required if the narrative is devoid of the joy that comes with generosity of spirit.

Setting out on duty alone

Sometimes we set off on a transition in ministry with little real enthusiasm and with only a sense of duty or obedience to motivate us. How far does that, alone, take us? Sometimes duty, by the grace of God, moves into a desire to be more than obedient. To desire what God desires is a form of obedience. Duty, having been transformed by love for God and loving response moves into desire. Desire, by the same reciprocated love, moves into delight, not least our delight in our reconciliation to the path we find ourselves upon. As the psalmist puts it: 'I long for your salvation O Lord, and your law is my delight' (Psalm 119.174).

Being reconciled to a situation means a positive acceptance of it; but acceptance is rarely something we come to in an instant. Acceptance vies and jostles with feelings and emotions such as resentment and regret, before it becomes a consistent condition with concomitant feelings of peace and joy. However, if a sense of reconciliation is reached through capitulation or resignation, one may be far less energized and this may lead to a state of ennui. In joyful obedience, in gratitude and generosity of spirit lies the way to positive acceptance. In the words of Dag Hammerskjøld: 'For all that has been – Thanks! To all that shall be – Yes!'

6

Transitions in Later Life

In this chapter we consider whether discerned decisions we make in later life are approached differently from those made when we are younger. We might say that we grow in maturity and wisdom and that we learn from past experiences, including past traumas and mistakes. One would hope so. We have discovered, however, that no two decisions are quite the same and so there are times when past experience or learning does not assist us much as we would like.

We cannot say that senectitudinal decisions are any less momentous than early life decisions. It is true that decisions about which A level courses to take can colour what further educational pathway we tread, and that may influence career choices. It is true that decisions about whom to marry or a decision to embrace the celibate life have far-reaching consequences, but who is to say that just when we think we are past major upheaval God will not call upon us to do something life-changing? We have only to turn to the Bible for examples of God doing just that. Abraham and Sarah, for example (Gen.18.9–18) became parents in old age and established a dynasty which several world religions, to this day, consider as foundational. Moses, too (Deut. 34.5) was still working until his death at the age of 120!

What then is the relationship between age and ministry (and for the purposes of this book), ordained ministry? If we say that it has an age-related cut-off point we suggest a theological and ecclesiological position of functionality. If, however, we deny the significance of advancing years on competence and capability, with no checks or balances, the Church could be said to be insensitive to personal need on the one hand, and irresponsible on the other. There is, too, a fine line between encouraging the use of gifts and learning, valuing acquired wisdom and experience, and exploiting ministerial resources generously offered.

Although there is an inclination to think first of older ministers retiring from active ministry, we should not overlook the fact that older women and men are offering themselves for ordained ministry. There are now many pathways to ordination and not all pathways are blocked against the older candidate. Just as some in their sixties are preparing for retirement from ministry, others are being ordained deacon and priest. Transition into ordained ministry in later years brings its own challenges, but it can bring to the mission and ministry of the Church a new lease of life founded in wisdom and experience.

Those who are responsible for their sponsorship, formation, training and deployment must exercise skill and sensitivity. They must ensure that all that the would-be minister has brought with them is valued and held along with new learning in a style appropriate to their needs and circumstances, so that best possible use is made of what they offer, to ensure that they are a senectitudinal blessing in the tradition of Abraham, Moses and others. Having acknowledged the gift of those who come to ordained ministry in later life, we consider now those who are engaged in transition into retirement.

Transition and retirement

I find myself wanting to write 'retirement' in quotes because my experience is that many so-called retired people are, by their own admission, as busy as they have ever been. Having crossed an institutional threshold, marked perhaps by the arrival at a milestone birthday, they may still be busy doing many of the things they did before.

Senectitude may be characterized by a change in perspective on God, faith, Church and life in general, and a change in how ordained ministry is understood and exercised. This is the time of life I will term retirement. To some extent the process will be driven by the rules of the institutional Church or the organization or institution to which one has been latterly accountable. Others may have turned their attention to new-found or recently rediscovered interests or to family commitments, courses, or causes. There may be a change of emphasis, a change of circumstances or income, but a change may not always be a rest! For some, retirement means the end of a significant piece of ministry, stipended or not, full-time or not, and the beginning of something else. Parish clergy, chaplains and other ministers in secular employment will reach a time when a significant change of direction is indicated or appropriate. For many of us, retirement is not synonymous with the end of ministry in holy orders.

In our reflection we have discovered that climate, context and circumstance all play their part in the experience of transition. We have discovered, too, that our individual vocational pathway has to be considered within the broader mission and ministry of the Church. Our vocational journey which began at our baptism and continues until we arrive in heaven, is characterized by chronological milestones, cultural norms, and pensionable age legislation. These need not be our main concern, but they do have a bearing on the transitions we make in later life.

We may reach a stage when, through physical or mental incapacity or disability, we are unsafe to practice some aspects of ministry. Some ministerial activity requires us to function as civil officers with responsibilities in law. In the exercise of these offices we may become a hazard to ourselves or to others. It may be that we find it increasingly difficult to assimilate change. Some ecclesial change may take us too far from our own theological understanding and belief. For all sorts of reasons, it may be time to lay down a significant ministry. In short, it may be time to go.

Here, then, we own retirement as an entity that can be viewed and experienced in many different ways. We consider it as a transition in ministry that presents us with decisions to make and problems to be solved, but also with opportunities to be grasped. We consider what might be different about this particular transition and what might be different about our discernment of God's will for us at such a time. We consider what might be different about the way we make decisions in later life.

In an earlier chapter we considered Janet and Geoff as they reflect on Janet's retirement from full-time ministry. We heard of their send-off from the parishes, but we didn't hear about the immediately preceding years, about what brought Janet to retirement.

Janet and Geoff's story: the prequel

Janet hadn't thought deeply about retirement until a letter came from the diocesan continuing ministerial education department inviting her and Geoff to a two-day residential event called 'Preparation for Retirement'. Janet had just celebrated her sixtieth birthday and was still deeply engaged with her ministry. She had, of course, given consideration to where she might retire and to how she and Geoff might live. Basic needs for shelter and provision would be met. In that she understood herself to be blessed. She knew that she could continue in post for many years yet but she had no great desire to do so and, in any case, she thought that would not be fair to Geoff who would be expected to retire from his occupation on his sixty-fifth birthday. As she and Geoff were much of an age, Janet had imagined that she would retire at 65. In this sense the decision to retire from her current form of ministry was determined by family considerations, by occupational retirement policy and by age. Where and how to live beyond retirement would be largely determined by market forces and income: aspects of transition largely out of their control.

It was only while attending the preparation for retirement course that Janet and Geoff considered what their prayers on the matter might be about. They did not consider it necessary to ask God if they should retire or even when they should retire. Janet mused that God did not have a strong view either way! It had not occurred to her that God might be working his purpose out through state and church policy on the matter.

One of the speakers on the course explored with them ideas of rest and refreshment. Janet and Geoff, like so many others, had 'borne the heat of the day' and should not feel guilty about taking time for leisure pursuits or for simply admiring the view. Janet found this hard to hear. For her, ministry had been about 'doing', every bit as much as it had been about 'being'. She smiled to herself when she remembered how often she had advised overly busy people that they were 'human beings' and not 'human doings'. She realized, for the first time, how much she had measured her own worth by what she had done, by what she had achieved, and not by who she is and by who she might yet become.

Preparing to lay aside one form of ministry without obvious prospects of another made her ask herself questions about her identity and her worth. It made her consider her broader identity as a child of God, as a Christian, as one of countless people whose vocation is to become who they were created to be, and to see that development as being beyond church or civil constraints of age or occupation. Janet (and Geoff) concluded that they were not retiring from anything of ultimate importance but without diminishing anything they had tried to do for the Lord in the work they had been given to do.

The two-day event on preparation for retirement came swiftly to an end and although neither Janet nor Geoff made little direct reference to it over the years that followed: they experienced something of a mind shift. Each in their vocation and ministry were no less busy and no less committed, but there was no question in prayer about what God might want from them next. They leaned into the inevitability of retirement from stipended ministry and paid employment and allowed themselves to consider their identity and worth in terms of who they are and not in terms of what they do.

Esther de Waal recalls how she first encountered the Benedictine tradition: how she was an extremely busy woman but how, later in life, she had more time and leisure to face questions which, formerly, she had been able to evade because of her busyness (1989, p. 14). Retirement removes some of the distraction from the questions in our hearts. It can be a time of thankful review and of regret. It can be a time to reflect on the choices we made over the years, to wonder if they were, in fact, God-centred. Keeping busy in retirement can be motivated by many things, including the fear of stopping to reflect and to wonder!

There are so many factors which shape who we are by the time the calendar or the Church Pensions Board or the state announces that we are to retire. Thank God, there is, as yet, no legislation to make us live in a certain way in retirement! The voices that tell us how to live are more likely to be the voices that taught us about work ethic or how hard work is rewarded and how leisure is sloth. Other contemporary voices tell us that some activity is good for us: some mental and physical stimulation will extend healthy life. Financial resources will, to some extent, circumscribe what we can do, disability will bring constraint.

It may be, however, that institutional rules (both ecclesial and secular) are God-given. They may be God's way of saying: 'rest now', but without a few robust scriptural accounts of God telling his people to take out a deckchair and sunbathe, some will find it hard to rest. For others, like Janet, this is the time to address that long-felt and deep desire to 'be still', to 'be' rather than to 'do', to witness to the 'Sabbatical God', to model the much-neglected seventh day tenet of created order. Modelling stillness among God's people is a gift and a privilege. Sylvia's story might illustrate this.

Sylvia's story

Sylvia is wheelchair-bound and is taken, every Sunday, to the church nearest her home by a kind neighbour. It is not the sort of church she had served in most of her life, but she is grateful for the lift and wouldn't feel she could ask her neighbour to take her several further miles to a church of her own tradition. She has a contemplative spirituality and now finds herself parked in the middle of a lively charismatic evangelical congregation. At first the congregants were welcoming. Then they were keen to 'minister' to her, praying that she would be healed of her infirmities. Later, when healing was not forthcoming (in the way they expected), they prayed that the demon which bound her to her wheelchair would be cast out. Sylvia remained still, prayerful and patient throughout. As time went by, many of the congregants tended to avoid her. She sensed this was because they thought she had let them down and had not co-operated with God's healing plans for her. Also, they were disappointed in themselves that they could not see her delivered from all that ailed her. Then, little by little, congregants began to seek her out for spiritual direction, for advice or to ask her to pray for them or with them. After several years of faithfully turning up, Sylvia had found herself with a new ministry based in stillness and prayerful presence.

Sylvia's retirement had been foisted upon her prematurely by disability. She had not stopped being a Christian or a priest. What disability and early retirement opened up for her was a fulfilling ministry enriched by having less distraction from focus on her deep relationship with God. In the busiest times of her life she had not been able to heed the call to the contemplative spirit within her. Now she could, and others were benefiting from it. Who she is and what she does bears witness to the Sabbatical God. One wonders how many older or infirm clergy see themselves in that way. One wonders, too, if younger serving clergy who find such a person as Sylvia in their congregation can discern the God-givenness of such ministry alongside their own.

In Western culture we are not good at valuing our elderly citizens for their experience or their wisdom, and the Church is ambivalent about it. On the one hand the growing numbers of retired clergy help support the Church's mission and ministry but, sadly, some serving clergy find them a threat and a nuisance. It was put to me, by a senior cleric, that to use the 'retireds' to cover absences or vacancies is to prop up an institution that is dead and should be given a decent burial. There may be some truth in that, but, clearly, ministry in retirement can be a blessing to the Church. Sylvia offers us a positive example.

Retirement with regret

When it comes to transition into retirement there are variations on a theme, and reconciliation to retirement is not always so positive. Some ordained ministry carries with it a certain profile, an entry into people's lives, and a voice in a community or in society at large. Some ministers find the loss of these things deeply painful and depersonalizing. Some, following retirement, never recover from that loss and some seek to recreate the sense of it through other causes and works of merit. On the other hand, some find retirement an opportunity to revisit interests long neglected, to enjoy more time with family or to enjoy some privacy in contrast to the 'goldfish bowl' experience of ministerial life.

But what do they seek to discern at this time? Is there a discerned decision to make or has it been made for them by the institution of the Church? Their prayer may be: 'I realize that the rules say I must leave this ministry now but, where to next, Lord?' Their prayer may be 'I am glad that's over, Lord. Please don't ask anything further, at least, not just yet!'

Is not our ministry both functional and ontological? To describe our ongoing ministry simply in terms of what we do is to give it functionality. Our ministry is not just characterized or identifiable as that of officiating at baptisms, weddings and funerals or leading Sunday worship. Before 'retirement' ordained ministry was more than that and, for many clergy, it continues to be more than that. If, in retirement, our value is defined in merely functional terms, we collude with secular commodification.

Happily ever after?

Some clergy do not wish to continue in active ministry once they have retired and there is anecdotal evidence to suggest that some clergy, once retired, not only cease active ministry but also stop going to church. Not everyone's story of ordained ministry ends 'happily ever after'. People leave ordained ministry for a variety of reasons. Some will have been hurt by those they sought to serve, others may have become disenchanted or deeply disappointed in the institutional Church. Some may have experienced a crisis of faith or belief while others may have found a new and fulfilling ministry in another part of the Lord's vineyard. A significant number of clergy, however, will want to continue to make a contribution to the life of the Church through the ministry in which they were ordained for life.

Age or infirmity is no measure of zeal for the gospel and a pastoral 'heart' may still beat soundly even if physical infirmity makes for difficulties, but there are other factors that can have a bearing on retirement. One comes across elderly clergy who have not made a healthy transition into retirement. Many had invested all their energy into their ministry and had not found time to pursue hobbies or interests that they could develop in later life. Some relate how they had found it difficult to cultivate friendships while in ministry. Relocating in retirement to a new and unfamiliar community has meant starting again with acquaintances out of which friendships can grow, but some find it easier than others to cultivate them.

Some retired ministers can feel rejected and lose their self-esteem. One elderly priest who has given many years to self-supporting ministry regularly laments that he can no longer preside at the Eucharist. He says: 'I can't get down, you know' (meaning he can no longer genuflect), 'and even if I could, I wouldn't be able to get up again!' To the suggestion that a monastic bow might replace the genuflection he responds: 'they wouldn't like it' (meaning the congregation would find that unacceptable). The ritual of the church he has served for several decades, a church that called for him to be ordained priest, cannot accommodate what he can offer. At the same time, he finds it impossible to compromise on the liturgical practice of a lifetime. A mutual acceptance of circumstance brought about by age and infirmity might bring him peace, but conditioning on his part and intransigence on the part of others has led to a lamentable and uneasy resignation.

Retirement and relocation

Although there are examples of clergy retiring happily in the benefice in which they had recently ministered, it is not thought to be good practice partly because it can inhibit a community from making changes and moving on in their vision as it unfolds over a generation. It can make things difficult for a new incumbent who seeks pastoral opportunities to build relationships and to serve people through their own gifts. This means that, for the majority of retiring stipendiary clergy, retirement will entail relocation. Self-supporting ministers, however, may be retiring from paid employment and may continue to live at the same address with no discontinuity to their ordained ministry, continuing to offer their ministry in liaison with other members of the ministry team, and according to the minister's changing circumstances or inclinations. Clergy ministering in chaplaincies, such as in schools, hospitals or prisons, may be subject to a retirement policy. Some will have been required to live in accommodation related to the role so they, too, will have to relocate. In this we are no different from millions of others who have to move on for one reason or another. In practical terms, for the most part, we just get on with it. In theological terms we know we have 'no abiding city' (Heb. 13.14) here on earth. As we reflected in Chapter 4, we have to be ready with our staff in our hand and our sandals on our feet (Mark 6.8–9), ready to journey on.

Redundancy and reorganization

At a time when dioceses are looking to make savings or effect pastoral reorganization an ordained minister may be standing in the way of organizational transition. It happens in many other organizations. A new structure is created in order to better support organizational goals. Roles are reshaped or redefined and one either has natural succession rights to one of the newly created jobs or one has to apply for one or more of them. Some posts become redundant and some people find themselves without a job. The Church, as an organism, as an institution, is not immune from this phenomenon. Many people like to think of the Church as 'counter-culture' and therefore not like the rest of society in the way that it deals with organizational transition. Anecdotal evidence suggests that the Church, which needs to continually reform itself for its ongoing mission and ministry, is not as adept as some secular bodies in caring for the people adversely affected by such organizational change. One hears accounts of duplicity and manipulation, of a lack of clarity and honesty that has catapulted lay employees and ordained ministers into unemployment or early retirement, with subsequent bitterness causing scandal that can bring the Church into disrepute. A church in transition will have consequences for individuals, but protocols for dealing with those affected by change embrace not only civil and canon law but the Christological commandment to love one another.

Disappointment and thwarted ambition

Ambition is not a word used openly in the Church. One does meet people who, privately, will share their ambition to play a significant part in the life of the Church. I suggest that every member of the Church plays a significant part, that no parts are more significant than others, but the word is also used to conceal a desire to attain diocesan and national roles and functions. When a prospective ordinand is asked about their calling they may say, 'I feel called to be a priest', but would they say, 'I feel called to be a bishop'? Yet, for some, this is the ministry they will find themselves exercising. They may say they had no inkling that their ministry would evolve in that way. Some clergy are open with trusted friends or colleagues about their ambition to serve in the episcopate, in a prestigious parish or in a cathedral post. Setting aside the concerns we may have about egotistical motivations for such preferment we can hear, too, a form of ambition that is seated in zeal and vision and the need for a bigger, broader or more influential platform from which to proclaim the gospel. This, too, is ambition but an ambition that God can work with and one which the Church needs if we are to function each according to our gifts. Here, we reflect on how thwarted ambition (of either the egotistical kind or the truly zealous kind) can impact upon transition into retirement. We might find it helpful to consider this under three headings:

First, there are those who have not found or been given the platform they long for but who have become reconciled to their disappointment or their unfulfilled dreams. They have been able to talk through these matters honestly with a friend, spiritual director, or spouse. If they reach retirement so reconciled or if they can come to that position soon after retirement, it can be so much easier to settle.

Second, there are those who not so much sought a larger-scale ministry or a prestigious post, but who had simply wanted recognition for what they had done, or had just wanted their bishop to remember that they were still alive! The longed-for affirmation (in human voice) may never come. There is a link between effectiveness and affirmation in ministry, and affirmation during service can be so much more valuable than affirmation delivered in a speech at one's retirement party!

Third, there are those who genuinely feel they could have made a more significant contribution to the building of the Kingdom, but feel they had been overlooked or undervalued. Here, gender disparity and prejudice as well as sexuality is not to be underestimated.

Exhaustion and resentment

Exhaustion at the point of retirement is a significant factor. It will rescue some from resentment: 'I would have liked to have done more, but I became too tired.' In others it will fuel resentment: 'I was so tired doing a thousand things that I didn't regard as appropriate to my ministry that there was no energy to pursue the things on my heart.' There is an argument that, compared with a generation ago, clergy are more likely to be exhausted at the point of retirement.

Transition and consequence

Transitions in ministry, as with life in general, are a series of beginnings and endings: times of holding on and of letting go, times when we test everything and hold fast to that which is good (1 Thess. 5.21). Testing the goodness of an idea, a proposal or a proposition placed before us requires us to be open to the possibility of all things, measured against what we know would be approved of by God. We look to the teaching of Jesus and the leaders of the early Church for guidance as to what is good and right and true. The commandments of God and the teaching that flows from them, as well as an informed conscience, self-knowledge and self-awareness, will guide us too. As we have explored in an earlier chapter intuition and our previous experience come together to test an idea, plan or proposal.

Further, we are not only distinctive individuals, we are members together of the Body of Christ. Our transitions, and all that is at work in the process and experience of them, is influenced by and accountable to that Body. We recognize that all transitions affect other transitions. There is some truth in the philosophical and cosmological notion that if I wave my hand in the air the molecules I disturb have a 'knock-on' effect right across the world.

It is too easy, when considering a transition in ministry, to lose sight of the transitions of others that have either precipitated our own or that will have consequences for others. How did that vacancy for an incumbent for the benefice of 'Tiddlypush-on-the-Mire' come about? What we might behold as a God-given opportunity has come about because the previous incumbent has moved on, retired or died. Less obvious will be the congregant who moves on to another congregation because they cannot stand the sound of our voice or the changes we have made since our appointment. Can we take responsibility for that? I don't pretend to have an answer but it is worth considering what role the Holy Spirit has played in our ministerial dramas, the narrative of which has written parts and roles for others to live out.

Clearly we will believe that the Holy Spirit was behind the vacancy at Tiddlypush-on-the-Mire. We felt inspired to apply for it. Affirmation came in various ways. A friend rang up and asked us if we had seen the advertisement in the Church press: 'Sounds like your job!' or 'It's got your name written all over it' are the kinds of comments we hear. We prayed about it and filled out the application forms. We prayed about it, and lo we were shortlisted. We prayed about it, and the interview went well for us, but we didn't give a thought to the other three candidates who had prayed about it and weren't offered the job.

Full of enthusiasm and convinced of the rightness of our appointment we might conclude that anything we do in the post will have the backing of the Holy Spirit. Hence we throw ourselves headlong into a programme of change and development and may hardly noticed the huge transitional agenda we are imposing on other members of the Body of Christ, some of whom are beginning to hold the view that we are asking, not so much under the influence of the Holy Spirit the disturber, but more in the service of life the disrupter or, worse, in the service of our own ego!

Appointment does not give us carte blanche to do *anything* we might decide we will do. There are, of course, some checks and balances. We may need a 'faculty' before throwing out the pews in favour of some nice comfy and moveable chairs. We will need the agreement of the PCC before we can make certain liturgical changes. Unfortunately, we can also lose the support of the 'body' to whom we minister even before its representatives, parochial and diocesan, have reached for the rule book; and yet, we will claim that we have the authority of the Holy Spirit. The New Testament Church could give us some tips on how to test our prophetic utterances transformed into an agenda of change. Of course, the Holy Spirit may be behind the idea, but the same Spirit may not recognize the methods we have chosen to employ in the outworking of it. Sensitive consideration has to be given to the affect, as well as the potential effect, of a transition into a new ministerial context.

We have reflected on a range of transitions in ministry. We have considered what happens at times of conscious transition, where there is desire or need for change and where a decision, or a series of decisions, need to be made. We have considered the processes by which we come to a conclusion about what to do or where to go next while wanting and needing to frame such decisions around God's will for us. We have thought about the way in which the Holy Spirit has inspired us, guided us and emboldened us and the way in which life events disrupt the status quo. There is one dimension to transitions in ministry that should not be neglected and that is:

The mystery factor

As we look back on our ministerial journey, we may well acknowledge that some transitions didn't make sense to us then, but they do now; other transitions continue to be shrouded in mystery as we ask ourselves, 'What was that all about?' We may aspire to know one day what it has all been about, but when we come face to face with God, we may forget to ask, because we have become lost in adoration! Holding a position of not knowing and of not needing to know the answers to questions of why and how our life's ministry took the tour it did can bring us peace.

The mystery of our little life is hidden in the mystery of God. As St Paul put it to the church at Colossae, 'Set your minds on things that are above, not on things that are on earth, for you have died, and your life is hidden with Christ in God' (Col. 3.3). To a great extent we have considered ministerial transition from a 'down to earth' perspective, but the source of our ministry is Christ's own ministry, and while Christ is to be found in the faces of the people we serve, he is also to be found in the heart of the triune God: a mystery in which we dwell. So what do we know about God? The answer has to be that what we know has been revealed to us in Christ. Supremely, what we know about God is that God loves us and that we are to love God back. This truth is the basis of our reflection in the next chapter.

7

Discerned Decision Making
Governed by Love

God is love

We have explored discerned decision making from a number of angles. Here, we reflect on it from the inside out. We look to the heart of it, to the fountain-head from which flows all else about it. In short, we look to Love not only as a verb but as a divine noun. Love is the very essence of God, yet God, as Love, is beyond our understanding, except in terms of our own experience of loving or being loved. The concept of God as Love, as described by the author of the Johannine epistles (1 John 4.16b) may be too awesome to fully comprehend, but if we reflect on our own experience of love we can catch a glimpse of it. Love, as God, is not a different kind of love to the love we experience. Love is love (Cardenal 2006). In the contemplation of Love we assume the position of mystic. In the outworking of love, in our response to Love, in loving service, we assume the position of moralist. The two are inseparable but, for the purposes of this reflection, we consider them, briefly, from those two positions.

Love's embrace

As mystics we dwell on Love for Love's own sake and behold it where we find it. For the mystic, love is the only reality but it is dynamic, changing shape and form continually while remaining ever the same. We are held by the God we know in Trinity. We are caught up in the dynamic of the Father, the Son and the Holy Spirit. It is a dynamic of vibrant love, and we are caught in the torrent of that love outpoured in the world. We are carried on its tidal wave and transported in its adventure. Times of transition are explicit occasions of awareness of the movement of Love.

In Chapter 1 we considered restlessness. Here we own the restlessness of love as Lover and Beloved seek each other out, desirous of a new adventure together. The Lover and the Beloved are a pulsating and oscillating organism. God's love courts our loving in a dynamic of reciprocation and that love is characterized by the gift of intellect, freedom and choice which gives us such dignity, but brings with it such responsibility. Our love for God urges us to be good stewards of the dignity we have been given, motivating us to discern God's will in the decisions we make. As Christian ministers we seek to serve Love as divine noun and to serve lovingly. Thus Love is the dynamic of all movement and transition.

The revelation of God in Jesus Christ encourages and inspires us. The apostle Paul reminds us that love never ends (1 Cor. 13), and John tells us that 'God is love and those who live in love live in God and God lives in them' (1 John 4.16b). God so loved the world and Jesus came to demonstrate to us the extent of that love (John 3.16). Jesus is Love incarnate. So profound a revelation is this that the early Church writers, like Paul and John, struggled to describe the significance of it and to define what that love might be about. No matter how we use language to describe love we will always be frustrated, for love cannot be fully defined or articulated even as God cannot be defined or known. How are we to love this God who so loves us? Anthony de Mello, a Jesuit spiritual guide, asks the same question:

> What does it mean to *love* God? One does not love him the way one loves the people one sees and hears and touches, for God is not a *person* in our sense of the word. He is the Unknown. He is the wholly Other. He is above terms like *he* and *she*, *person* and *thing* . . . To love God with one's whole heart means to say a wholehearted Yes to life and all that life brings with it. (1984, p. 34).

Tongue-tied by love, we let the Spirit of God articulate for us, in sounds too deep for words (Romans 8.26), vibrations of reciprocated love, of God's love for us spilling out in returned love for God and for our neighbour.

Loving response

As moralists we concern ourselves with how love behaves: with the quality of the love which pours out from the embrace of our love for God. We concern ourselves with love in action, in experience and in its absence from our everyday life. Paul (1 Cor. 13) attempts to spell out how love behaves, or at least how perfect love behaves. It is something to which we aspire, even though we are always going to fall short of perfection in this respect. Only God loves perfectly and God's perfect love for us attracts us and draws us in loving response.

Love cannot work in isolation. For the dynamic of love to work and to be fully expressed it has to be reciprocated. As Christians we model something of this not only by our declaration to the world that God loves us, but through our attempts to love and to serve our neighbour.

Love and discerned decision making

Love, the only reality, calls for a loving response from us, but we may ask ourselves how implicitly or explicitly central is love to discerned decision making. How is love interpreted? How is it to be lived out in ministry? If it is a healthy love, there will be a conduit of desire to link both the God of love and the love of one's neighbour. The healthy spirit may not, in practice, be particularly pragmatic (for all sorts of reasons), but there will be a deep-seated care for the displaced and in many, a yearning to be in that place with the displaced bringing a presence of love, of reaching out to the margins to find and serve love as well as the desire to find Love deep inside us. In other words, the search for love and the service of Love is both an inward and an outward journey. The desire to put love into action has always been considered key to spiritual growth. Sheldrake (1998, p. 198) reminds us that many of the spiritual greats (Augustine, Julian of Norwich, Ignatius of Loyola) made this point over and over again. Together with that striving for intimacy with God, those with a healthy spirituality will know, or will be open to finding out, how to respond appropriately to the needs of their neighbour. Authentic spirituality rests in God-centred and authentic humanity. It is something to desire and to strive for: a yearning for the wholeness of love.

The Cuddesdon Twelve on love and loving response

The experience of securing a curacy comes at a time when ordinands, through learning and formation, are exploring their understanding of the nature of God, of his mission in the world, and of the nature of the Church, its structures and strategies for co-operating with God in the building of his Kingdom. They seek clarification of the part they are to play in the outworking of God's plan for them, asking: 'Does this curacy offer fit into my understanding of God's explicit and implicit macro plan and my understanding of my micro role in that plan at this time?' Many of them implied that even if they could not come to an unqualified affirmative response at the time of asking, they accepted that if other stakeholders had come to a positive conclusion they were prepared to trust that discernment. Most of the curate respondents accepted that, with hindsight, it had been God's will for them at both a macro and a micro level. They were encouraged to articulate what was behind and beneath their offering of themselves for ordained ministry. One respondent replied:

> This is something I keep asking myself! This is a really tough one and is probably as hard to answer as the 'voice your vocation' part of discernment, because the feelings that motivate me now are the same ones that led me to this point. There are no words that can adequately describe the motivational pull of a call from your Father. From that call the conversation begins

and a flame begins to burn more brightly than it has ever done before and *a love that cannot be found on this earth becomes the centre of all you do*. My motivation deep down is to remain in the conversation and to share that same love with those that God draws me towards.

I found that, in every interview, if I adopted a gentle but persistent Socratic style of questioning and gave respondents long enough to find words to express themselves, each one of them was left with just one word that summarized their motivation: LOVE. A few were embarrassed to use the word, reluctant to appear 'fluffy' or 'soft'. Others thought it so central and so obvious as to be taken for granted. One would hope that it would be so central and so objective, because ministry is lived love; but it seemed that although it might be obvious, the theme of love, as the source and essence of the motivation for ministry, needed unpacking. What follows, therefore, is an interplay between the shared reflections of respondents and some further authorial reflections upon this theme.

In Chapter 3 we heard of Susan and her experience of the process of securing a curacy: at the centre of it, a difficult decision to be made. She reflected and knew, in her heart, that Moortown was not 'right' for her, yet she carried a burden of guilt, because she had taken the action of accepting a curacy nearer her parents. Susan was concerned that her action contradicted God's plan for her, but does God have a plan? The answer might be 'yes', but it appears to be a bigger plan than Susan imagines. God's plan is to govern by love, and Susan's part in that plan is to love God and her neighbour as herself (Mark 12.29–31); but is there not a category of loving concern that should be more explicitly defined? It comes somewhere between love for our neighbour and love for ourselves. Susan's love for, and the honouring of, her father and mother falls into this category.

Love of neighbour, self and self-plus

There are those who are extensions of us, whose lives are so bound up in ours that even mundane everyday decisions affect their lives.

For the purposes of this book and to aid reflection I have termed these 'self-plus'. Susan made a loving choice in deciding to minister nearer her parents, and God blessed that choice with signs of the decision being 'right'. Susan has yet to experience life as a curate in Neartown, and no doubt her experience will raise more questions and dilemmas, and the cycle of reflection, discerning, deciding and taking action will continue as her experience unfolds, but she began with a love-based decision and God will honour that.

Susan demonstrates a model of theological reflection reminiscent of Green (2009, p. 42), as her deliberations begin with the experience of the curacy-securing process, through an exploration of what might be 'right'. She explores the validity and credibility of the offer over and against her sense of calling. She needs to reflect on God's will for her and her sense of duty to her parents before she can respond to the curacy offer, but does this model do justice to the extent of her rumination? Green (2009, p. 103) offers us a 'secondary cycle' that allows a thicker and richer theological reflection process as intuition, exploration and 'new witness' (fresh insight?) aid the reflection. Using the device of a secondary cycle it is possible to make more explicit a thicker description of discerned decision making within the process, setting both the primary and the secondary cycles in the context of God's love and our loving response. These two cycles, when placed together, form a figure-of-eight model with the stage of decision making at the point where the two circular cycles join. Central to the upper cycle is the truism: 'God is love' and central to the lower cycle is the injunction: 'Love God, neighbour and self-plus'. (See figure 1).

When we make a discerned decision, we have already been round the upper cycle of praxis (action) giving rise to reflection on our experience of life and of God in that experience. Then comes a dilemma, the beginnings of a need to make a decision, which gives pause for reflection. That reflection takes us off to the secondary cycle as we identify the problem, weigh the pros and cons, seek advice and consider our options. We check if a potential decision feels right and meets the need. We may, or we may

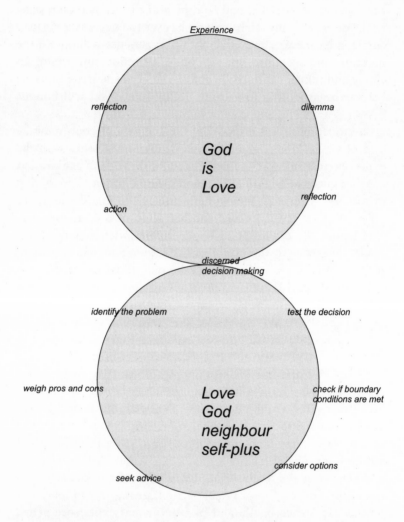

Figure 1: A model of theological reflection and discerned decision making*

© Raymond Tomkinson

not, have the facility to test or to try the option before we make a commitment to it. We can only work with whatever inspiration or aspiration, facts and feelings we have at the time. What might be an appropriate outcome in one time, place or circumstance may not be appropriate in another. We can only really measure the decision by asking the question: 'Is this the most loving thing to do for God, for my neighbour and for myself-plus?'

It can be argued that we are, in this way, adopting a situationalist position. Fletcher (1966), who pioneered our contemporary understanding of situational ethics, attests to the centrality of love to decision making. He asserts that, for a situationalist, 'only the commandment to love is categorically good' (p. 26). He cites Tillich and others (p. 33) in holding that

> Christian situationalism is a method that proceeds, so to speak, from (1) its one and only law, agapē (love), to (2) the sophia (wisdom) of the church and culture, containing many 'general rules' of more or less reliability, to (3) the kairos (moment of decision, the fullness of time) in which the responsible self in the situation decides whether the sophia can serve love there, or not.

Susan has learned something about God, about love, about discernment and decision making. She will learn that Love resolves and Love absolves. It will inform and colour her praxis: there will be a practical outcome to the process which will be more than the securing of a curacy post. At the heart of her ministry there will be love as gift (1 Cor. 13) and as fruit (Gal. 5.22) of the Holy Spirit. Susan is typical of respondents for whom love is the wellspring from which flows all else; but what is the epistemological significance of scriptural warrant regarding God's love? I turned to John the Evangelist, whose Gospel and epistles are peppered through with references to love. He tells us that 'God is love and those who live in God live in love' (1 John 4.16b): a text we considered briefly in Chapter 1. For John, living in love and living in God are synonymous. If we are to follow this teaching, we must recognize that all our living is bound up with God's love, and that includes the decisions we make to align our loving response with God's love for us.

The love of God *for* us calls for a response *from* us. As Dewar puts it (2000, p. 52):

> a task or activity, engaged in for the love of it, by which others may be enriched or released: something you do as a freely chosen expression of your nature and energy; something that expresses the unique essence of yourself which God calls *out from you*.

Our purpose is to love and to serve God, to participate in God's life and purpose and to share in God's initiative in bringing in his Kingdom of love. Personality, gifts and life experience shape who we are. This is what we offer to God in love. What, then, lies beneath and behind our loving response to God's love for us? Is it based in dutiful obedience?

We love, John reminds us, because God loved us first (1 John 4.19). Jesus, in his affirmation of the lawyer's summary of the Mosaic law (Luke 10.27), brings a sublime and awesome imprimatur to this revelation, giving it the status of law. We have the Christological commandment to love one another (John 15.17), but how can God legislate for our loving response? Surely love has to be freely given, but in his command to love one another Jesus reminds us that it is not enough to love God: love must be expressed, lived out, in love for others, with Jesus' own example of love before us. For John, the love of God is supremely revealed in the suffering and death of Jesus. We can expect that if we are to model our loving on that of Jesus, our loving service of others may well entail sacrifice. We must be cautious here to differentiate between, a notion that if it hurts it must be 'right' and something being 'right' but which might entail pain or sacrifice.

It should not be sacrifice which drives ministry but love, which, to be fully expressed, may well require sacrifice. We may ask if loving sacrifice is freely given in the service of God, our neighbour and ourself-plus, or does love *compel* us? The paradox here is that God invites yet Love compels. St Paul illustrates this well as he relates how the love of Christ (*αγαπή*) controls him (RSV); impels him (*συνέχει*[1]), urges him on, constrains him (KJV) by *holding him back* from self-centred boasting and living: not against his will, but because 'we have decided (*κρίναντας*) that one (Christ) has died for all' (2 Cor. 5.14).

I am reminded of a work by the Spanish artist, Francisco de Zurbaran (1598–1664) whose painting, *The Bound Lamb*, brings a poignant reminder of the self-offering of Jesus, the Lamb of God. In the context of this study one can see the ordinand in preparation for a life of sacrificial ministry: the bonds that tie the lamb are, paradoxically, liberating bonds of love. Remember the verse which so inspired Michael in Chapter 4:

> Were the whole realm of nature mine,
> That were an offering far too small;
> Love so amazing, so divine
> Demands my soul, my life, my all.[2]

I believe, however, that besides the imperative of the Christological commands, there is an *invitation* to serve God. Love beckons.

Love and desire

Our inclination towards one kind of service or another is born out of our perception of our gifts, our personality, and our life experience, but the inclination surfaces through desire. We desire to love God in return for his great love for us. We desire to be poured out in the loving service of others. God, who loves us, wants to give us our heart's desire. We have only to ensure that our desires honour him. For Rolheiser (1998, p. 7) such desires are rooted in *erotic* love as distinct from *agapeic* love, but nonetheless God-given. One of the Cuddesdon Twelve stated: 'It is where I want to be. God said: "tell me the desires of your heart"

---

1 The word means to be impelled or driven along a course from which one cannot deviate.

2 'When I survey the wondrous cross.'

and so I did.' I asked the respondent: 'What *are* the deepest desires of your heart?' He replied:

> Where I am totally in the right place doing what God wants me to do, and it's safe and secure for the children where they're at. What is underneath that? Wholeness and then *shalom*; doing the right thing and everyone's got it. All in the right place.

We find ourselves returning to a familiar theme but, this time, in the context of Love and loving response. God delights in his children and he delights in our efforts to please him and he delights in our delight. What delights us motivates us, and motivation is a key factor in sustaining a work begun. So, God speaks through our sense of duty, through our wholesome desires and through the things that delight us. If we listen to anyone's account of their journey towards fulfilment in the service for God, these elements will be present to a greater or a lesser degree. The following account may help to illustrate the movement from duty to desire to delight that some respondents described.

Charlie's story

Charlie, an ordinand, and his wife, had agreed that they did not mind where they served so long as it wasn't in Crabtree. Before training for ordained ministry they had both worked in Crabtree, and they had hated the place. It was rough, even dangerous in parts, and they did not want their children to live there, even for the three years of the curacy. When the time came to consider Charlie for a curacy appointment, his bishop invited him to look at Crabtree! Being a good-hearted fellow and wanting to please God, but with prayerful protests to God on behalf of his children and his very sceptical wife, they went to look at the curacy in Crabtree. They began to bargain with God. 'Well, yes, Lord, but not this suburb or street or school.' By the time they found the location of the house in which they would live (bigger and better than they had expected), in the street where they would live (a tree-lined avenue) and had met the prospective training incumbent (with whom they resonated well) and had heard of all that God is doing in Crabtree, they were sold! It felt right.

Duty, desire and delight had melded wonderfully with obedience, faith, hope and love. Did God want them to go to Crabtree, or would he have blessed them wherever they had gone if their intention was to love him and serve him to the best of their ability? I don't know. This is theological reflection, not theological answers! As people of faith we live with many unanswered questions, but assurance that we have made the right decision helps if we are to proceed, wholeheartedly, with a course of action decided upon. Our deepest motivations, based in love for God, for our neighbour and for ourselves-plus, may not be sufficient to determine action. We need to assess if we have 'got it right'.

'It felt right'

Let us return to how respondents described how they felt having made a discerned decision. 'It felt right', is the best position they could come to. The ministerial setting of the curacy captured their imagination. It seemed that the skill-set required was in place, or was achievable in preparation for carrying out what was required. The motivation and the energy were there to sustain the interest and the performance. It seemed as though it would be life-giving. It brought a sense of joy or excitement. Practical arrangements fell into place: difficulties or barriers were overcome. It felt right.

'It felt right' is, however, a subjective statement. It does not mean it *was* right. It allows the possibility that though it felt right it was, in fact, 'wrong'. It was a mistake. It was not what God intended at all! Vanstone (1977, p. 81), in a chapter about the 'response of being to the love of God', asserts:

> The response of nature is that a thing should be that which it was to be: that, out of the precarious endeavour of creation, it should 'come right'. If creation be the work of love, then there is always the possibility that that which is created may 'come wrong'. That it should 'come right' is the response in which

love becomes triumphant: that it should 'come wrong' the response in which love becomes tragic.

Getting the decision wrong?

We try to get it right but what would getting it wrong look like, feel like? I know of a priest who moved to a parish where nothing he did seemed to work. He had a really tough time there. His ministry put a huge strain on his marriage. His health suffered. He lost sight of his gifts. He was in despair. He moved to another parish and 'it felt right'. His health improved, his ministry flourished, his marriage was restored. Did he get it wrong by going to his previous parish? How did his experience of that parish inform his ministry in his subsequent parish? Did he get it right then because of the previous tough experience? Perhaps we can never truly get it wrong if our motives are to love God, our neighbour and our self-plus, because God, who is Love, meets us in *situs* and redeems what he finds there, including our well-intentioned decisions. Can a situation be said to be of God if there is no discernible love in it? The only real questions in testing out a discerned decision might be whether or not Love is honoured and served by a decision or the outworking of it.

Love: the only reality

How do the decisions we make fit into reciprocal love? Could we not say the only significant difference between secular and Christian models is the conscious dimension of the discernment of God's loving interaction with us as we work through a dilemma? Cardenal (2006) would argue, however, that every human soul, Christian or not, at the depths of their being, longs to respond to God's love. If he is correct, then in *all* decision making there is an unconscious desire to do the loving thing: something which honours God. Cardenal (2006, p. 3) asserts: 'We cannot rest till we find God. Only he can satisfy our heart and the enormous love that is in us with all the force of universal gravity. Towards him all creatures strain.' He goes on to declare (p. 55):

The voice of the Lord is existential not verbal. It does not sound in our ears, or in our minds, but deeper, where he is present, in our deepest self. His call makes us discontented and sick of everything. He does not call us by words, but by events, circumstances, by reality.

Vocation then is reality seeking and finding Reality: love seeking Love.

God and the detail of call

Dewar (2000), argues that our calling is entrusted to us, but he questions whether God gives it to us in such detail 'like a flat pack wardrobe waiting to be assembled by us, with or without specific instructions for its assembly' (p. 1), or if his gift to us is 'a compelling love and it is only when we discover the most fulfilling way to respond to Love that we discover our vocation?' For Dewar, vocation is 'doing what in your heart of hearts you love to do' (p. 6).

We may be clear about the generality of our vocation to love and serve God and our neighbour, but to what extent does God involve himself in the particular? Is it that people with certain skills (or interests) or with a particular personality (or disposition), and as a result of certain life experiences, offer themselves for ordained ministry and then God blesses the offering? Having received the offering made by us, does God then commission us to go to a particular location and to serve there? In other words, does he guide us in a general way, through all he has made us to be, and then leaves the detail of deployment entirely to his Church, asking only that the Church makes best use of the offering received and blessed by him?

Imprint not blueprint

I do not hold that there is a grand 'blueprint', an overall detailed and predetermined plan, only a timeless 'imprint' of love. Imprint means 'to recognize another as parent or object of habitual trust' (the Shorter Oxford English Dictionary). God gives gifts: inspirational and aspirational capability, vision, courage, wisdom, zeal. The Church, trusting to God, applies its collective spiritual and material resources to decide who to employ, engage or utilize and to deploy its human resources, lay or ordained, for the furtherance of its mission under God. I hold that God expects the Church to make appropriate use of all knowledge, wisdom and experience: both intra-ecclesial and extra-ecclesial, eschewing nothing just because it appears to emanate from a secular source.

The discernment process, as explicit and implicit search for the will of God, is applicable to the whole of the life of the Church and is applied extensively in ministerial transitions. Crucial at every stage in the process is the sense of call – essentially an invitation rather then a summons – yet Love compels, and a corporate consensus of such a call is enough for many to accept the call as the authentic voice of God. It is not a call to the individual alone: it is in the context of a call by God to the whole Church, evidenced in a pulsation of corporate and individual responses as God calls, and the Church seeks to make sense of that call. Fundamentally, it is not a call to lay or ordained ministry but a call to love, to live for Love.

Where does that leave the Cuddesdon Twelve? As they considered a curacy offer they sought to make a loving response to a loving God. Love and compassion for God's people urged them on but it was, in addition, a call to love which embraced the needs of family and friends. Even the priority given to the need for compatibility with the incumbent shows a deep desire for a milieu in which love and loving-kindness can flow in both directions. Respondents demonstrated, also, a need for a theological and liturgical framework in which the love of God could be most fully experienced and expressed.

Love sets us free

Freedom of choice is a gift of Love and it is closely likened to a freedom to decide. The test for whether a discerned decision is the will of God is whether or not it brings a sense of freedom: to draw closer to God, closer to one's neighbour in whom God dwells, and closer to a sense of being oneself, a recognition of God in us. Perhaps that translates as 'It feels right'. Nash (1999, p. 163), referring to the four cardinal virtues in Greek ethical thinking, cites Augustine of Hippo offering, as a Christian thinker, a corrective:

> Temperance is love keeping itself entire and uncorrupt for God; fortitude is love bearing everything readily for the sake of God; justice is love serving God only, and therefore ruling well all else, as subject to man; prudence is love making a right distinction between what helps it towards God and what might hinder it.

Another much quoted reflection of Augustine summarizes the relationship between being and doing; responding to the God of love in the general and in the particular of our calling: 'Love (God) and do as what thou wilt . . . let the root of love be within, of this root can nothing spring but what is good.'[3] Where there is potential to demonstrate or to receive love, such a place is mission territory because God's mission is to love us into his Kingdom. That is why Augustine could declare: 'Love (God) and do as what thou wilt', because if Love is the imperative 'what thou wilt' is what God wills.

We end this chapter with Susan poised on the threshold of ordained ministry. Susan is now free of her sense of guilt and is 'at peace' about the choice of curacy she has made. Blessings abound. She is excited about her future ministry as details emerge from the benefice of pastoral opportunities and a desire among God's people there for her gifts, learning and life experience. She senses she is free to serve God because love has bound her. She has learned with Augustine to 'love and to do what thou wilt'. Susan struggled, as we all do, to articulate love and loving response, to vocalize her vocation. Communicating and articulating in discerned decision making is the subject of the next chapter.

---

3 From the Epistle of St John, Homily 7.8; on *Nature and Grace* 70 (84) and on *Christian Doctrine* 1.28 (420).

8

Articulating the Vision

In Chapter 4 we heard of Michael and his long-held sense of call to religious life. We heard how he kept his thoughts to himself, fearing the reaction of his parents to his aspiration. Sometimes our thoughts are best kept to ourselves until we have inwardly rehearsed them a little and got them into some kind of articulable shape. Even then, we may find it difficult to articulate matters close to our heart. We may be intimidated by the person with whom we need to share such thoughts. Others may be so much more articulate than us, and we can feel daunted by their verbal dexterity. Their interlocutorial style may be overbearing: they may not be good at listening or they might misunderstand. They may not give us time to pour out our half-thought-through ideas. If the person is a stranger we may be quite wrong about them and find them to be a good listener and reflector of what we have said, showing empathy, patience and understanding. Nevertheless, by the time we meet with that stranger, especially one who has power to open doors to the realization of our dreams, we can feel tense, tongue-tied and emotional.

What we discover, however, is that vocalizing our sense of call, even haltingly or in a jumble of words and phrases helps us to know and to hear more clearly the voice of God. It is not uncommon for someone to approach me and to say something like: 'I don't know where to begin. I know that what I am about to share with you will come out in a confused heap. Please excuse me if I ramble a bit.' As they throw their thoughts into the space between us it is my privilege to join them in the heap and to help them to articulate their thoughts and feelings. Their 'God-speak' and mine may be different, their theological perspective widely different from my own, but we come together as two human beings who love God and who want to make sense of what is at work within us. We come together in the presence of the Lord and, rather like the two disciples who walked and talked together on the road to Emmaus in the company of the risen Lord, 'our hearts burn within us' (Luke 24.13–35) as we let God help us to order our thoughts and the articulation of them.

The language of discernment

Much discernment happens in dialogue: in exploring with an another the possibility of a transition, a move, a change in ministry. The language or languages we use in that dialogue have the potential to be a vehicle for the voice of God. Much will depend, however, on how well we understand each other's acquired and conditioned language and our dialect within the language of the Church.

No God-speak?

There is a stage in the process where the talk is all about the practical arrangements, the terms and conditions of service, the packing and the removers. In conversational terms God takes a back seat. The concern comes when God is not mentioned at any stage in the process, from reading of the vacancy in the Church press to the installation in the parish! To be fair, it may be that such conversation is taking place between intimates and confidantes or that the God-givenness of a situation is just that: a 'given' that needs no articulation. However, it does appear that the day-to-day 'business' of the Church can go on with scant reference to God.

The voice of God and human God-speak

The language of God is the language of love. The language of vocation is the language of loving response to Love. Perhaps we feel that the language of love has been hijacked by sentiment or by cultural conditioning. The reader may recall the ordinand who couldn't use the language of love because it was too 'soft', too 'fluffy'. Fortunately, the language of love is not only verbal. It is the language of deed and action: of suffering and of sacrifice. God's supreme articulation of love is in the passion, death and rising of our Saviour Jesus Christ. His words from the cross are valuable to us and they articulate something of the grace and mercy of God. The image of Christ crucified for the salvation of the world is an iconic communication of love. Notice how St John records: 'God so loved the world that he *gave* . . .' rather than 'God so loved the world that he *said* . . .'! The full articulation of the Christ event is more than the verbal proclamation of the good news of salvation. God's love in action speaks more articulately than any words we use to try to express the wonder of those actions, but infinite love cannot be fully articulated within the constraints of human vocabulary. We are grateful, of course, to those who, over the centuries have tried to express the inexpressible, but a number of questions remain: What is the language of God? How does God speak? Does the Church universal have a language or are there many dialects, making it difficult to converse among ourselves? Do we have our own personal God-talk? What if there is a mismatch of voices? Does God also use a secular vocabulary? Why are we afraid of it? In reality we hear, within the Church, language we might associate with secular organizations. Who is using the language of truth and integrity?

Language and theology

How we 'hear' God will depend, to some extent, on what we think God is like. Our theology gives us a perspective on God and from that comes a vision of how we should respond to God. That vision shapes into a call to a ministry which will, in its outworking, articulate, wordlessly at first, our response to God. That wordless articulation seeks a vocabulary to express the call or to explain it to those whose ministry it is to test it, or to nurture it to fruition. Our vocabulary, which has gradually developed since infancy, finds itself in a new infancy as we explore new concepts of God, as our life experience teaches us about God and the world in which God is sought and found. Exploring a transition in ministry involves being open to learning a new vocabulary of discerned decision making. Seeking and finding, knocking and finding doors opening, or not (Matt. 7.7, 8) requires a new listening and hearing, and a new articulation.

Secular vocabulary and church-speak

We use the language of human resources with words such as 'vacancy' and 'job'. Such words still grate in the ears of some ministers. Phrases such as 'value for money' have grown up alongside a growing correlation between stipendiary ministry and parish share commitments. Many clergy are immersed in secular organizations and enterprises bringing presence and a prophetic voice, helping to turn priorities to reflect gospel imperatives. We have to learn the language of the people with whom we work, but without 'emigrating' from the core values of the gospel.

We speak the language of the kingdom but with a variety of dialects, our God-language having been nurtured in a particular tradition. When we come together in community, in celebration, in congregation we represent the diversity of the Church in theology and ecclesiology, but we also reflect the Babel-like language of the Church universal.

Transitions in ministry and in language

Making the transition from secular employment to ordained ministry can be difficult for Christians who had always understood their work to be vocational but which carries its own technical or esoteric language or jargon. As we navigate our way through the deep waters of discernment we may carry with us many years of language conditioning. This can make it difficult to express ourselves to seasoned travellers in the ocean of the Church. As one ordinand put it: 'It has been like going for a job interview in a foreign country. There is the language as well as the culture to cope with!'

For those who have had extensive experience in a secular working environment the language of that occupation will continue to colour the articulation of vocation and ministry. Those we serve may find this helpful as we 'speak their language' and demonstrate a connectedness with the world around us. Those who continue in secular employment, in self-supporting ministries, for example, become proficiently bilingual and offer a valuable gift of interpretation as they fluently articulate the voices of the one to the other. I am sure we would like to believe that there is no real distinction between the language of the Church and the language of the world, but that would be like saying that there is no difference between England and America. To George Bernard Shaw is attributed the observation: 'England and America are two countries divided by a common language.'

In addition to decision-making styles discussed earlier there will be preconditioned problem-solving styles and expectations of how organizations function, how hierarchy is understood. Early transitions in ministry may find us still learning about the Church's distinctiveness and difference in culture and language compared to previous secular organizational experience. This learning may be commensurate and coexistent with learning about diversity and difference within the spectrum of Church theologies, ecclesiologies and language. As one priest reflected: 'When I was ordained I had to learn, and learn quickly, to use "Church-speak". I now use ten words when, formerly, three would have been adequate!' To this we might add 'profound Church-speak': the more rarefied the language the more profound it can seem. There is, too, a value placed on rarity that it does not always deserve. One hears this so often at meetings. The one who speaks rarely is often accorded a wisdom in direct relation to the sparsity of speech. It is only later, on further reflection, that the content is revealed to be less wise than was thought!

The Church likes to think of itself as counter-culture but it does not stop us importing something of the very culture we seek to change; and this includes the language. On the other hand, secular organizations have, for decades, used language we thought of as our own. Words like 'mission' have given rise to the phrase 'mission statement'. I heard it in the public sector long before I heard it in church! Do we seek to theologize everything because we want everything rooted and grounded in God, or do we sometimes theologize things in order to obfuscate them: to bamboozle or to prevent others from realizing just how inadequate we feel?

Non-verbal communication

This chapter is about how we articulate our sense of call to a transition in ministry to those who will be affected by it or whose ministry it is to help us discern God's will for us and for the wider Church. Space does not permit a full exploration of the importance of non-verbal communication in our discourses, but a brief reference here may suffice. Communications experts (Pease 1981 et al.) tell us that some 70 per cent of our language is non-verbal. We are, of course, careful in our interpretation of non-verbal cues: as we can misinterpret them and make wrong assumptions. We may say we rely on instinct, a subject we touched upon in Chapter 3, but instinct is sometimes no more than the reading of non-verbal cues and listening to our own reaction or response to those clues. A churchwarden, following an interview for a new incumbent, frustrated all the other members of an interviewing panel by raising an objection to the candidate's appointment as incumbent on the grounds that 'there was just something: I can't put my finger on it'. The appointment went ahead with disastrous consequences. With the benefit of hindsight, the churchwarden was enabled to articulate what they had been unable to express adequately at the time of the interview. It transpired that the non-verbal cues did not match the verbal responses the candidate made to questions: the truth of the matter being directly opposite to their verbal responses. Isn't hindsight a wonderful thing?

In the story of the two disciples on the road to Emmaus (Luke 24.13–35) consider not only the verbal exchange between the two disciples, and between them and Jesus, but also the non-verbal cues: the actions such as stopping, walking companionably, non-verbal signs of grief, hearts burning within them, sitting down, breaking bread. The risen Lord was recognized, initially, by his non-verbal behaviour! This passage from Scripture is worth exploring further.

Emmaus road: dialogue with Christ, listening together

The story of the two disciples on the road to Emmaus offers clues to meaningful dialogue in the presence of God. Dialogue, as a vehicle for understanding the will of God, is dialogue in the presence of the risen Lord. Always in such conversations, be they formal interviews or quietly exploring possibilities with a family member or a friend, Christ is present: recognizable in the words and action of the other and, sometimes, by the hearts that burned as the realization of possibilities emerge. Creative thinking is thinking in the presence of, and under the influence of the Creator God. As we seek to find words to express our deepest desires and aspirations, the Word of God is with us. Our deepest heartfelt love for God and our desire to love back in the service of God and of our neighbour is fired by the presence of the Holy Spirit.

We recognize, too, the importance of joint listening for the Holy Spirit and a waiting on the Spirit for both inspiration and articulation. Companionable silence, which is distinct from an excruciating silence experienced by one or other, can afford an opportunity to reflect, to rephrase, to digest, to pray for inspiration, guidance or illumination. Affording each other a little silence can make space for God to get a word in.

Articulation in the language of the Bible

The language of the Bible is set in a time and a culture: the vocabulary of the times. Metaphors we use now are not necessarily the same metaphors as those used by Jesus. How, today, would we describe the Kingdom of Heaven? Would we still refer to a mustard seed or to a king throwing a party? The language of the Bible is also the language of dreams, visions, signs and symbols. It is the language of parable. When it comes to discerning God's will through scriptural warrant we recognize that translations through several languages and through idioms, and the fast-changing nature of language itself, have influenced how we receive Bible truth.

When we seek scriptural warrant we might quote verses or passages that have 'spoken' to us. By that we mean that we sense God's voice behind the words: even words originally addressed to a nation, we appropriate as a personal message in an attempt to articulate the inarticulable deep inside us. But is scriptural warrant always enough to discern the will of God in a transition?

Ted's story

Ted recalls how he had prayed about a move from parish ministry to hospice chaplaincy. On the basis of his experience of visiting parishioners in a local hospice and being singularly unimpressed by the ministry of the chaplain there, he began to think how he would 'do things differently'. For him there was not nearly enough direct reference to Jesus and precious little 'ministry' in terms of prayer and the laying-on of hands. He challenged the chaplain about this and received a well-considered response that testified to the sensitivity and grace of the chaplain. Ted prayed about this and asked the Lord for a 'word' from Scripture to guide him. The next morning, at Morning Prayer, he was 'convicted' by: 'I solemnly urge you: proclaim the message; be persistent whether the time is favourable or unfavourable; convince, rebuke, and encourage, with the utmost patience in teaching' (2 Tim. 4.1–2). Without further consideration, and 'under obedience to the Spirit' Ted decided to apply for a position as chaplain in a hospice in another part of the country. He made an informal visit and met with the hospice director and a senior member of the nursing staff. They showed him round, and they described the ministry of their chaplain who had now moved on. Ted outlined the approach he would take if he were appointed. He noted that the senior nurse was wearing a tiny dove emblem in her lapel. 'Ah!' he exclaimed, 'I see you, too, are a Spirit-filled Christian! Perhaps I could just say that God has promised to grant me my heart's desire, and my heart's desire is to minister here!' Somewhat taken aback, the nurse had no words to say in response except: 'Oh, I see.' Ted was not shortlisted for the post, and he took the rejection very badly. He telephoned the hospice and spoke to the senior nurse. He told her that he thought they had got it wrong, and that God's will was being thwarted. She listened calmly before responding: 'Clearly, Ted, you have a great deal of zeal and enthusiasm, but I too prayed for guidance in the appointment of a new chaplain. God's word to me was: "I know the plans I have for him but they are not for here and not for now."' Ted was stunned into silence. The shortlisting committee comprised health care professionals of explicit faith, of implicit faith and of no faith at all. Ted's referees included his bishop and a parishioner. The discernment that he was not the right person to appoint as chaplain for the hospice was unanimous. Had Ted received feedback from a member of the hospice team who did not profess a Christian faith, Ted might have been unable to 'hear' the appraisal of his unsuitability. Armed with his seemingly impregnable divine authority, he may have wanted to argue a case for being offered an interview. It was much more difficult for him to argue with another Christian's equally confident 'word from the Lord'. Whatever the perspective and whatever the articulation of the shortlisting committee, it felt 'right' to them that he wasn't appointed. For Ted to grow through this experience of rejection and to find his niche in ministry there would have to be a dialogue of another kind: one in which love, openness and gentle honesty would bring Ted to a clearer understanding of his gifting.

It is tempting to appropriate Scripture to underpin our desires and ambitions. Taking a passage from Scripture that is an account of prophetic words to God's people, to a nation, and applying it to our personal circumstance is sometimes a sincere attempt to articulate a genuine sense that God is guiding us through our decision making. We read what we need to read, hear what we need to hear. When a verse of Scripture at Evening Prayer jumps out of the page at us and makes sense of a dilemma with which we have wrestled all day, we cannot dismiss it as merely coincidence.

We may prefer to call it a God-incident, but there is always the danger that, in reading what we want to read or hearing what we want to hear the scripture that seems to jump out has indeed been wrenched out by us to justify a decision we have made, a stance we have taken or to justify the way we have behaved. I commented earlier on how we need to exercise caution in the interpretation of body language: that we should 'read' such cues in the context of all the other evidence and information available. It is similar with scriptural verses that jump. When we are trying to discern the will of God we should read them in the context of discussion, dialogue, advice, sign and testing, taking into account all the evidence. It seems to me that God rarely offers one sign or word only in response to our prayer for guidance. In Chapter 3 we heard of Susan and the sign in the car-park that indicated that she should say 'No' to a curacy offer. Susan did not read that sign out of context. She queried the validity or God-incident validity of the sign. She would not have made a decision based on the sign alone. Like finding a place on a map, we need more than one coordinate to ascertain the location. We triangulate points of reference. Although this term refers to a technique used in surveying and navigation, the Trinitarian undertones and possibilities are not lost on us. St Paul's advice on the testing of prophecy comes to mind: 'Let two or three prophets speak, and let the others weigh what is said' (1 Cor.14.29).

Beryl's story

Beryl recalled how, during a selection conference for ordained ministry, a selection adviser had pushed and pushed her to express the nature of her call. She remembered returning angrily to her bedroom, opening the Bible and finding a passage that said what she had been trying to say about her calling. She wrote the selector a note, quoting the text she had lighted upon and, at the next opportunity, shoved it into his hand. The adviser said nothing to her. It seemed to her, with hindsight, that he was more in search of her passion than he was of an articulation of her sense of call to ordained ministry. Either way the discovery of the text was epiphanic and opened up for her an articulation of her call.

Telling the story again and again

Articulating the vision, the desire and the calling to those who need to hear it, to test it and to help it to fruition is not something one does on one occasion only. The story has to be told again and again. Although this can seem tedious, there is merit in it. We considered earlier how retelling the story can help us to become clearer about God's will for us; but it can also help us to articulate our sense of call in a way which makes it easier for others to comprehend.

Malcolm's story

Malcolm felt called to ordained ministry. He had shared his thoughts and aspirations with his parish priest, and, over the following months, he had met with diocesan vocation advisers and a DDO. At each stage he had told the story of how he had come to faith and how he had become aware of his 'call'. Now he was meeting his diocesan bishop. The bishop said: 'Malcolm. This is how it is. God calls, we respond, and the Church tries to make sense of it.' Leaning back in his chair the bishop continued: 'Tell me your story.' Malcolm, glancing at the file on the bishop's lap, toyed for a second with the idea of replying: 'but I have told my story at least four times already!' He thought better of it and began to relate an account of his journey thus far. In one sense, Malcolm was beginning to find it easier to tell his story. Phrases he had used before, he used again and again; but in another sense he was finding it increasingly difficult to articulate his sense of call. Words and phrases seemed trite and hackneyed. He noticed that alongside familiar phrases, repeated at each interview, different dimensions and aspects emerged as each successive interviewer had gently probed, seeking further detail or clarification. These interviews with people who were genuinely interested in getting to know him and in hearing about his sense of call were a series of dialogues out of which were coming fresh insights into the God who seemed to be calling him and fresh insight into himself. Only with the benefit of hindsight did Malcolm realize that the interview process was a key part of the discernment process: the Church trying to 'make sense of it'. The bishop was encouraging and told Malcolm that he was prepared to send him to a selection conference (Bishops' Advisory Panel), so that his vocation might be further explored. With a gentle smile the bishop, having picked up Malcolm's non-verbal cues when asked to tell his story, said: 'Malcolm, you will have to tell your story a few more times yet.' Following a few moments of silent prayer the bishop blessed Malcolm before they parted. On reflection, Malcolm recalled how affirmed and strengthened he had been by the bishop's gentle insight, by the silence and the blessing he had received. Telling his story had not been a problem to Malcolm after that. Malcolm's account of the early exploration of his vocation is heartwarming, encouraging and inspiring, but the experience for many others is that it is less than straightforward.

How stress can alter behaviour

Times of transition, whether forced upon us by circumstance or entered into willingly and excitedly, can be times of stress, and stress can affect our behaviour. At each stage of the discernment process there can be so much at stake that we can feel such an intense pressure that it changes the way we usually behave. We may become under-confident or overconfident. We may become under-assertive, over-assertive or even aggressive. In an effort to 'say the right thing' we can hear ourselves saying precisely 'the wrong thing'.

A colleague commented that some ordinands are rather 'flat-footed' when it comes to dealing with diocesan officers or prospective training incumbents. He felt that ordinands would benefit from advice on how to be assertive in negotiations over, for example, working agreements or housing needs, thus avoiding reactions caused by a lack of sensitivity or diplomacy. The standard advice is: 'be yourself'. 'Yes, of course,' we reply; but we are left wondering which 'self' is the one to be! Should it be the patient and tolerant self who can appear amazingly stress-free? Should it be the reflective self that would rather express the longing in a sigh 'too deep for words' (Romans 8.27)? Should it be the outgoing, energetic self, the pulpit self or the pastoral one-to-one self? As a result of stress or fear that we may not be known for who we are, or valued for all we can offer, we may exaggerate ourselves. We may behave defensively, guardedly, weighing every word so that we appear ponderous and wiser than we are. We need to listen carefully to what is being said to us, what advice or guidance is being offered, but in that listening we may forget to respond, even non-verbally, frozen to our seat, leaving the adviser or guide wondering just who we are.

Enabling someone to express all that they are and all that is on their heart and mind is both a gift and a skill. Thankfully, worthy women and men in roles serving the deployment of ministerial resources are, for the most part, blessed with such gifts. Unfortunately, 'bad' experiences become well-known, whereas the countless times that situations, interviews and negotiations are handled well go unheralded. The reader may know the age-old customer service maxim: 'Those who receive good service will tell three others, while those who receive bad service will tell seven others.'

Clare's story

Clare's story is one of a conversation that went badly wrong, but also one where the challenges that rose from the ashes of it led to a fulfilling outcome. Clare met with her sponsoring bishop to discuss a curacy offer. She had been worshipping in her sponsoring diocese for eight years prior to training for ordained ministry. She was pleased to be offered, on completion of her ministerial training, a title post in the diocese; but she had deep reservations about accepting it. The post was a few miles from her sponsoring parish. She had made many friends there and had kept in touch with some of them and living and working near by would afford an opportunity to sustain those friendships. When she talked them through with a fellow ordinand, she realized that her reservation was about 'place'. Prior to moving to that area, Clare had a high-flying job in the media. She had worked long hours and had lived a hard and fast lifestyle. Eventually she buckled under the pressure of deadlines and a demanding boss. We might say she had a nervous breakdown.

She moved to the countryside and got an administrative job that was undemanding and well within her capabilities. She made a good recovery and began to rise through the company to a junior executive level. She attributed much of her recovery to God and the church community in which she had found herself. Through that whole traumatic experience had come a vocation to the priesthood. Clare realized, however, that her sponsoring diocese had been a place of recovery, of healing and renewal. When she looked around her she saw the faces and the landscape that had been part of that recovery, but she saw, also, the distorted and pain-filled vistas of her former pathological scenario. The ministering angels jostled for position in her mind's eye with the dark demons of the past. She sensed that she needed to move on in order to minister effectively.

Being an able communicator she believed she would have no difficulty articulating this to her bishop. He, however, had difficulty in hearing it. He would not accept her reason for rejecting the title post and suggested she go away and return when she had come up with a better reason. Angry and distraught, Clare wrestled with this suggestion and came to the conclusion that she was actually being asked to tell a lie: to fabricate a reason not to accept the curacy offer, one which would be acceptable to the bishop and the diocese. The whole incident gave Clare pause for thought about God, the Church and the ministry.

She continued to explore the offer, meeting the proposed training incumbent and key people in the benefice. She was taken to the one-bedroom flat that would be her home and workbase in the parish. With the best will in the world, it was woefully inadequate. Would they consider housing her more appropriately? No, they would not! Clare returned to the bishop to tell him that she could not accept the curacy he had so kindly offered her, because the accommodation was unsuitable for her needs. The bishop understood completely and said that since all other curacy posts in the diocese were now filled, he would, reluctantly, release her to seek a curacy elsewhere. This she did and continues to thrive in her ministry.

Difficulties with articulation

Some ordinands, reflecting on the journey from the first sense of call to the commencement of training, relate how the journey has been life-giving. They relate how they have learned so much about themselves, about God and about the Church. They relate how the articulation of their call has changed and is still changing. Some ordinands describe, however, that they are still unsure whether they are 'doing the right thing', hoping that the years of training will bring them to a more confident frame of mind. Here they rely on all those who have been involved in the discernment process. They have not heard the voice of God like Samuel in the Temple (1 Samuel 3.1–18), but they hear the voice of God in the wider Church. They journey in faith in the company of the faithful, trying to 'make sense of it', continually revising the script of their vocational articulation. For many the articulation gradually requires fewer words. Many reach the point where a deep sigh accompanies the words 'It just feels right': a recurring phrase in the articulation of discerned decision making in ministerial transitions.

Although Francis Dewar (2000) had his doubts, ordinands *do* reflect deeply on the particular of their call, but some have difficulty articulating it, seeking language to express it which is neither woolly or fluffy. We explored in Chapter 7 how the language of vocation is the language of love and how it is difficult for some to use such language confidently. The absence of this from their articulation should not be interpreted as evidence of no heartfelt, love-drawn call. Some need encouragement to make connections between Love who calls and we who respond in love and service to God, our neighbour and ourselves-plus.

I commented earlier on God's communication of love through action: through the giving of his Son in sacrifice. Those who are involved in helping others to a discerned decision about a transition in ministry will be looking and listening for an articulation of a spirit of self-sacrifice, of generous self-offering. Although some might be under the illusion (quickly shattered!) that ordained ministry is an easy option, most people who offer themselves for ministry are aware that some degree of sacrifice will be required. None of us can predict what it will ultimately cost, but entering into life in Christ through Christian discipleship is entering into an unwritten contract: it is a 'signing up' to the possibility that such discipleship could be costly. Therefore, as we discern that God is drawing us deeper and deeper into the ministry of his Son, and that he is asking more and more of us in terms of personal commitment and sacrifice, our very offering of ourselves for ministry and our perseverance in it as we make one transition after another, is testimony, in itself, to our desire to love and to serve God and our neighbour.

Sharing doubts and concerns

Sometimes we find it difficult to share, or we believe it is inappropriate to share, the doubts and the turmoil we experience during a transition. If we choose to keep such things to ourselves we may not realize that other stakeholders are having similar thoughts or concerns. We may deprive ourselves of helpful assistance, reassurance or advice. Many may become too preoccupied with the problem and lose all perspective on it. If, however, we are the sort of person to tell everyone every detail of every concern, we may lose support and sympathy. Not everyone else can cope with such a level of disclosure. Not disclosing, however, can court disaster.

Brendan's story

Brendan interviewed for the post of team rector and was offered the post. Having returned home he began to have serious doubts about it. At first, he kept his reservations to himself. He reasoned that they were rooted in nervousness about the role he would be undertaking. Having no immediate family and not wishing to air his doubts with churchwardens or parishioners in his current ministry, Brendan spoke at length about his doubts only to his spiritual director. She urged him to voice his doubts to the church-wardens of the prospective ministry or to discuss them with the archdeacon. She knew he had a good relationship with his bishop and encouraged him to share his thoughts with him. Brendan de-cided to 'ride it out' reasoning that the doubts were not significant enough to be heeded.

Two years later Brendan's doctor told him he must take extended sick leave. He had become clinically depressed, and, through per-sonal neglect, he had become malnourished and prey to all man-ner of physical ailments. It was only then that Brendan had a frank and open conversation with the churchwardens. It was only then that they told Brendan they had been in doubt about his ap-pointment from the beginning, but had been afraid to share their reservations with the archdeacon for fear of having to experience an even longer interregnum.

Discernment through the written word

Some discernment in decision making takes place through the written word. By this I mean that information is displayed in an advertisement in the Church press or on a diocesan website, and the language used will make a difference to who responds. 'Dy-namic, energetic priest sought for exciting new church plant ini-tiative' will attract a different applicant from 'Gentle, diplomatic and patient priest sought for newly formed multi-parish benefice comprising ten parishes of diverse churchmanship.' A cartoon, of course, and the personal specifications need not be entirely mutu-ally exclusive, but if there are quiet stirrings and a minister senses a need to move on, this may be the first intimation of a possible direction. Advertisers, therefore, have an awesome responsibility.

Reading the signs

One is unlikely to find formal reference to what has been called the 'dark glasses and raincoat run': another name for the incog-nito and informal visit to a possible place of ministry to 'get a feel for the place'. This 'feel' might include reading the church noticeboard or the displays in and around the church telling of activities and initiatives with which the church is engaged. One curate told me that he based his decision to accept a title post almost entirely on what he gleaned in this way. 'It told me so much,' he remarked.

Documents sent to prospective candidates, commonly called, 'parish profiles' vary enormously in the quality of the information and in presentation. Some relay details of the nearest railway station or golf course but neglect to mention the mission, spirituality or outreach of the benefice! While acknowledging the danger of information overload, in the context of all the data which helps in discerned decision making in a transition in ministry, the potential value of the written word should not be underestimated.

What next?

We have searched our hearts and weighed in our minds the possibilities of a transition in ministry. We have shared our thoughts with friends, family, spiritual director, soul-friend or colleague, articulating our deepest thoughts, ideas, vision and concerns. We have asked questions, made enquiries, volunteered, applied for the post, been open to an approach from Church authorities to consider a different ministry. We have prayed about it, asked God for a sign or simply placed our trust in God for the outcome. We have consulted Scripture, heard a word in a reading or psalm. We have done our best. We are ready to make a decision! What happens next? We consider this in Chapter 9.

9

Readiness to Journey On

The decision is made! Announcements have been made. Now begins a time of adjustment and of waiting. We stand like Janus, the Roman god of gateways and doorways, who is usually depicted as having two heads: one looking back and the other looking forward. At a time of transition we look back on what we have learned and experienced: we look forward to what lies ahead (and not necessarily in the eager, optimistic sense of the phrase!)

We think of the people we have come to know and love and the ones who were hard to love. We think about how much or how little we will miss them. We consider what we were able to do or to contribute and what we would have liked to have done or completed. People around us are saying how sad they are to see us go or saying nothing unkind but can hardly contain their relief that we are going!

We look ahead to the ministry that awaits us. We recall the brief meetings we have had with a few of the people to whom we will minister. Already, people are asking us to comment on this idea or to come to some event so that the people can meet us. Meanwhile, there is so much to do in preparation for departure. There may be family members to consider, jobs or schools to find. For some there will be a need to sell and to buy a house, for others it is a move to a house provided with the ministry. In either case there will be property agencies or departments with whom negotiations must take place. It can be a stressful time and tempers may flare. The upheaval can be exhausting spiritually as well as mentally and physically. There may be moments when we completely forget we are going anywhere or moments when we feel that sense of nervous excitement as we remember what was so attractive and potential about the transition we have agreed to undertake. Whatever the colour of the experience, transition in ministry has begun!

Throughout the discernment process we have learned to trust in God, trust in the other stakeholders, in the judgement of our friends and families. Trust has been implicit and explicit but not without its occasional absence. We know that God's people are people of faith. As we travel in ministry we travel hopefully, trusting in the guidance of the Holy Spirit. 'For surely I know the plans I have for you,' says the Lord, 'plans for your welfare and not for harm, to give you a future with hope' (Jer. 29.11).

We may experience 'middle of the night' negative thinking which can undermine our confidence in the future and our trust in God or in the people to whom we are being sent. We may lose confidence in the decision we made, and that initial and attractive vision of the future may disappear. When 'middle of the night' thinking takes place in the middle of the day things just get worse. It is as if the Lord is asking if we can trust him when the vision is turned off and when we don't hear a sound of reassurance. The words of a nineteenth-century hymn, 'Trust and obey' come to mind. These words were written by John H. Sammis in 1887 and were inspired by a young man at an evangelistic event led by Dwight L. Moody. The young man humbly owned that he knew very little about the Christian faith but was prepared to 'trust and obey':

> When we walk with the Lord in the light of His Word,
> What a glory He sheds on our way!
> While we do His good will, He abides with us still,
> and with all who will trust and obey.
>
> Trust and obey, for there's no other way
> to be happy in Jesus, but to trust and obey.

To paraphrase an expression used by Michael Ramsey: there are times when we trust; times when we want to trust, and times when we want to want to trust. We might have our doubts about a transition to which we have committed ourselves but doubts that are worked and prayed through can bring new strength to faith. The opposite to faith is not doubt but certainty and we are a people who live by faith and not by certainty.

In a time of transition we are rather like passengers waiting in the departure lounge of an airport. This trip is likely to entail a one-way journey. We think of the people we have left behind, the familiar haunts, the places we shopped or played, the vistas we enjoyed. The jobs left undone or partly done. As we wait we think of all that lies ahead: immediate practical considerations taking up all the space in our heads and in the conversations with our fellow travellers.

If there has been time and space to reflect at this stage of the transition, and staying with the airport analogy, it might be worth considering the baggage we are carrying with us into the new adventure. Perhaps we are carrying more than we need: more than is good for us.

Shedding the baggage

It might be time to reject the baggage of 'self-doubt' and the voice that tells us, derisorily, that we are not worthy of our calling or not up to the job. In one sense we are not, but to dwell too much on that truth is not helpful: it is a sin against the Holy Spirit. There is a need to stop apologizing for who we are. Accepting our call is one way of rejecting the burden of self-doubt. There is a need to rely, now, on all those who have discerned and affirmed it.

Some of the baggage is the burden we may still be carrying as a result of past tensions and disputes that had negative and destructive consequences that went beyond the usual healthy arguments that show that we are all individuals with an opinion of our own. We ask: 'What has been destructive and will be more so if it is not put aside?' This baggage includes burdens of sin, of being sinned against, of hurting and being hurt, of resentment, which has accumulated over the years. Is it time to review all that we are carrying? Is it time to offload some of it: to let go of it and to mark that letting go sacramentally or ritualistically?

Among the many tasks that need to be done in preparation for a move is putting paperwork in order. There may be documents that would be best shredded. A shredder can be quite a useful vehicle for a ritual of quietly and prayerfully offloading some of the baggage. Writing notes, in the presence of God, about that which has been burdensome, hurtful and damaging, or regrets about sins of commission or omission and then shredding the notes can be quite effective. The contents of the shredder can be emptied into a composter so that it can turned into something good for the soil. The words of another great hymn come to mind:

Low at his feet lay thy burden of carefulness:
High on his heart he will bear it for thee,
Comfort thy sorrows, and answer thy prayerfulness,
Guiding thy steps as may best for thee be.[4]

It is time to let go of the unnecessary: to let go of burdens of regret or guilt. Christians are not meant to bear burdens of guilt for very long. At times of transition we ask God to help us to appraise all that we are carrying and to help us to identify baggage that we could well do without. This may not be an easy or a pleasant thing to do, as some things from the past can stick to the lining of our spiritual suitcase and may be difficult to prise out, but we shed what we can before we move on.

Shedding baggage at a time of transition is part of a continuing process of shedding baggage. It is necessary to do it over and over again because we are likely to be helping other people to shed their own baggage (what's good for them is good for us!) and we need greater carrying capacity so that we can help others to carry what they must carry. At each transition in ministry (and often in-between) baggage-shedding is good practice. If we do not jettison what we should not be carrying, we will never travel well in ministry. Somewhere in the midst of the upheaval of transition it is good to find a little quiet space where we can give the exercise of spiritual and emotional baggage-shedding its rightful place. For some of us that place is the sacrament of reconciliation.

---

4 The second verse of the hymn: 'O worship the Lord in the beauty of holiness!' J. S. B. Monsell (1811–75).

Travelling light: essential luggage

Having addressed the matter of excess baggage, the next consideration as we prepare for the journey into a new aspect of ministry
is what constitutes essential luggage. I have always admired those
travellers who take the absolute minimum with them. When I am
at an airport, queuing to check in my baggage, I may find myself
standing behind a couple of travellers dressed in jeans and a light
top and sunglasses, a little rucksack slung nonchalantly over one
shoulder. What have they got in there? A spare set of underwear,
a toothbrush, a clean T-shirt, a mobile phone? Me? I need a suitcase just for my medication, plug-in mosquito thingy, sun creams,
lotions and potions! All necessary luggage!

When Jesus sent his disciples out to proclaim the good news of
the Kingdom, he told them to take the minimum with them. We
travel light in order to be free to go where we are needed but also
so that we have capacity to help carry the burdens of others. Part
of the discipline of ministry is to check regularly, however, that
the burdens we are bearing are appropriate burdens: that they are
truly ours to bear, that they are legitimate luggage. Jesus, said:
'For my yoke is easy; my burden is light' (Matt. 11.30). Here the
'yoke' is not meant to be burdensome but to be a guide (to prevent the beast slipping off the road into a ditch) and the burden
of Christ, who is not burdensome at all, is no weight at all! The
correct burdens have no weight and neither do the burdens that
we carry in the right spirit.

Sometimes we carry the burdens of others with such bad grace,
saving our energy for projects that excite us. I once saw a small
child emerging from a supermarket carrying a very large box. I
think it was a space station set. He was excited, and though red
in the face from the heaviness of the box, he would not let go of
it, would not let his mum help him with it. A week or so later I
saw the same child and his mother emerging from the same supermarket. The mother was pushing a heavy trolley laden with
purchases. Teetering on the top of the trolley was a box of cereal.
As it began to slip off the trolley, she grabbed it and asked her
small son to carry it beside her to the car. He reluctantly cradled

the cereal box but huffed and puffed and moaned as he trudged beside her. Gone was the delight he experienced as he carried the heavy box of toys!

In order to make room for bearing the burdens of others we need to ensure that our essential luggage is truly essential. But what might that include? It should include the love of God in our heart: the knowledge that God loves us infinitely and that we are infinitely lovable. It will include Christ in our heart (remember, he is no weight at all). He carries not only our burdens but carries us too. We carry the word of God on our lips. We bear the sacraments of the new covenant. In our hand we carry the staff of authority: Christ's authority vested in his Church, vested in us. Our feet are shod with the beautiful gospel of peace (Rom. 10.15).

Baggage, luggage or – 'buggage'?

Is it really that easy to let go of spiritual and emotional baggage and to travel light with essential spiritual luggage only? I doubt it. That is why I have come up with the word 'buggage'. It is term I use to classify the baggage that is still in transition, caught somewhere on the carousel of life. It is baggage we are still trying to offload: burdens of our own and the burdens of others that we carry for a while. It includes the baggage we would dearly love to lose but which keeps coming round on the carousel and, no matter how much we ignore it, still comes back. As it comes round we flick over the label, checking that it is still ours and that we must own it a while longer. It is the baggage of unease, of things not resolved, of forgiveness given or received but restitution possible and not yet achieved.

Buggage cannot be carried in the arms: it would be too restrictive and would handicap our ministry. It is best left on the carousel or if it must be toted around then it is rested on wheels to ease our onward journey. Those wheels are kept oiled with prayer. Our prayer is one of trust in God to repair what we cannot repair: to resolve what we cannot resolve: to forgive what we want to forgive. We look to God for reassurance that, ultimately, all will be well, and all manner of things shall be well (Julian of Norwich). Meanwhile, the reality is that we all carry buggage. Some buggage is not our own but that of others, including the burden of those things shared with us in absolute confidence. Fortunately God reduces the size of that burden to a microdot making it easier to bear but (mercifully) difficult to recall.

Transition: beginning and ending

When does a transition begin and end? I suggest it begins the second we conceive the vision of it, and it ends when we are un-selfconsciously getting on with it. Between the beginning and the ending of a transition in ministry we labour in the service of the vision we have been given in trust. We will go forward in confidence that God will bring good out of our discerned decisions made in our attempt to love and serve God, our neighbour and our self-plus.

A key part of trusting is believing in ourselves. Whether we are on the threshold of ordained ministry or whether we have been in ministry for many years, we need to remind ourselves, from time to time, that our call has been tested and affirmed by the Church. If we find ourselves in transition we do well to remind ourselves of the confidence we came to in accepting a new ministerial context and the confidence others have in our calling and ability to take it up. There is a fine line between self-effacing modesty and false modesty, the voice of which asks for more and more affirmation that we are doing the right thing. One can become addicted to reassurance. Humility is truth, and if the truth is that we are confident that, with the help of God, we can undertake a work in God's service then we own that and allow the inner voices of self-doubt to have their say, thank them politely for their opinion, check out any possibility of a grain of truth in what they say, and then get on with the task in hand!

Transitions in perspective

There is more to transition than moving to a new ministerial location or to a different aspect of ministry. Transition can be about a change of disposition, of outlook or of orientation. It can be about a change of heart. Conversion is a transitional experience. Sometimes such transition is a prerequisite to a transition in the way we have reflected on in earlier chapters. Transitions are a series of death and rebirth experiences. They are micro-experiences of the birth, death, rebirth cycle of our life. If we are to be faithful to God there will be a desire to continually die to self that we might live for God and for others. Transitions require generosity: the willingness to 'lay down our life for our friends' (John 15.13). Sometimes, however, there is greater generosity, and a more profound laying down of one's life by *not* moving on. Here the transition is one of the heart where one has worked through the death of a restless spirit: a desire for pastures new (greener or not!) and rebirth we will experience in the acceptance of an abiding place, in a work, in a ministry.

Transitions: an eternal perspective

There is one transition which we all face sooner or later. It is the transition from life to death and beyond. The ultimate relocational transition is into heaven. It seems not only neglectful to exclude it from this book, but there is also a danger that our reflections on decision making in ministerial transitions might lose that broader context of our life in Christ. Putting our reflections into an eternal context reminds us that our lifelong transition is into Christlikeness, into the image and likeness of God, into wholeness and holiness, not only so that we can more effectively carry out Christ's mission and ministry in the world, but in preparation for continuing to live our life hidden in God in eternity.

Transformation as transition is threaded through all our ministry. It is a transition God has been working in us all our days. Sometimes we have been aware of it and sometimes not. Pastoral encounters or personal experience can make us reflect on that final transitional phase, causing us to review our priorities. Such pondering on the ultimate and eternal context of our ministerial lives puts all our decision making, discerning, agonizing, our hopes, aspirations and dreams into perspective. Paradoxically, seeing the eternal heavenly context of our ministry brings us down to earth.

All our resources, poured into our ministry, run in parallel conduits of activity and passivity, of apostolate and contemplation. They continue and converge in the infinite love of God.

What are we to conclude about transitions in ministry? First of all that transition is a constant feature of life. We are always in transition. There is no stasis. Even if we feel settled or content emotionally or spiritually, physiologically we are in transition. By the grace of God, the ultimate transition is one of being:

Changed from glory into glory
til in heaven we take our place
til we cast our crowns before him
lost in wonder love and praise.[5]

---

5 The final verse of the hymn: 'Love divine, all loves excelling'. Charles Wesley (1707–1788).

Bibliography

Barth, K. (1960), *Church Dogmatics* III, Edinburgh: T & T Clark.

Bell, J. (2005), *Doing Your Research Project*, Maidenhead: Open University Press.

Blaiklock, E. M. (Tr), (1983), *The Confessions of St Augustine*, London: Hodder & Stoughton.

Butler, G. and Hope, T. (2007) (2ⁿᵈ edition), *Manage your mind: The Mental Fitness Guide*, Oxford: Oxford University Press.

Cardenal, E. (2006) (2ⁿᵈ edition), *Love: a Glimpse of Eternity*, Brewster, MA: Paraclete Press.

Carr, W. (1985), *The Priestlike Task: A Model for Developing and Training the Church's Ministry*, London: SPCK.

Cocksworth, C. and Brown, R. (2002), *Being a Priest Today: Exploring Priestly Identity*, Norwich: Canterbury Press.

Croft, S. (1999) *Ministry in Three Dimensions: Ordination and Leadership in the Local Church*, London: Darton, Longman and Todd.

Denscombe, M. (2007), *The Good Research Guide*, Maidenhead: Open University Press.

de Mello, A. (1984), *The Song of the Bird*, Garden City NY: Image Books.

de Waal, E. (1989), *Living with Contradiction: Reflections on the Rule of St Benedict*, Glasgow: HarperCollins.

Dewar, F. (2000) (2ⁿᵈ edition), *Called or Collared?: an Alternative Approach to Vocation*, London: SPCK.

Drucker, P. F. et al. (2001), *Harvard Business Review on Decision-Making*, Boston, MA: Harvard Business School Press.

Etzioni, A. (1989), 'Humble Decision Making', *Harvard Business Review* 67, Issue 4, pp. 122–6.

Fletcher, J. (1966), *Situation Ethics: the New Morality*, London: SCM Press.

Giles, R. (2006), *Here I am*, Norwich: Canterbury Press.

Gillham, B. (2000), *Case Study Research Methods*, London: Continuum.

Green, L. (2009) *Let's Do Theology: Resources for Contextual Theology*, London: Mowbray.

Gross, R. (2001) (4th edition), *Psychology: the Science of Mind and Behaviour*, London: Hodder and Stoughton.

Hammersley, M. (2000), 'The Relevance of Qualitative Research', *Oxford Review of Education* Vol. 26, No. 3/4, pp. 393–405.

Hammond, J. S., Keeney, R. L., Raiffa, H. (1999), *Smart Choices: A Practical Guide to Making Better Decisions*, Boston, MA: Broadway Books.

Hayashi, A. M. (2001), 'When to Trust your Gut', *Harvard Business Review* 79, Issue 2, pp. 59–65.

Heller, R. (1998), *Making Decisions*, London: Dorling Kindersley Limited.

Heywood, D. (2011), *Reimagining Ministry*, London, SCM Press.

Hoch, S. J., Kunreuther, H. C. and Gunther, R. E. (eds) (2001), *Wharton on Making Decisions*, New York: John Wiley & Sons, Inc.

Julian, J. D. (1982), *A Dictionary of Hymnology, Setting Forth the Origin and History of Christian Hymns, Together with Biographical and Critical Notices of their Authors and Translators*, London: John Murray.

Kuhrt, G. W. (2000), *An Introduction to Christian Ministry: Following your Vocation in the Church of England*, London: Church House Publishing.

Leonard, C. (2009), *Holding On and Letting Go: Reflections, Stories, Prayers*, London: SPCK.

Lewis-Anthony, J. (2009), *If You Meet George Herbert on the Road, Kill Him*, London: Mowbray.

Marshall, I. H. (1980), *The Acts of the Apostles: an Introduction and Commentary*, Grand Rapids, MI: Wm B. Eerdmans Publishing Company.

Martin, J. (ed.) (1990), *Curate's Egg: the Inside Story of What a Curate's Life is Really Like*, Crowborough: Highland Books.

Nash, R. H. (1999), *Life's Ultimate Questions: an Introduction to Philosophy*, Grand Rapids, MI: Zondervan.

Pattison, S. (2000), *A Critique of Pastoral Care*, London: SCM Press.

Pease, A. (1981), *Body Language: How to Read Others' Thoughts by Their Gestures*, London: Sheldon Press.

Percy, M. (2006), *Clergy: the Origin of Species*, London: Continuum.

Pritchard, J. (2007), *The Life and Work of a Priest*, London: SPCK.

Ramsey, M. (1982), *Be Still and Know*, London: Fount.

Robinson, A. B. and Wall, R. W. (2006), *Called to be Church*, Grand Rapids, MI: Wm B. Eerdmans Publishing Company.

Robson, C. (2002) (2nd edition), *Real World Research*, Oxford: Blackwell.

Rolheiser, R. (1979), *The Restless Heart*, Denville, NJ: Dimension Books.

Rolheiser, R. (1998), *Seeking Spirituality: Guidelines for a Christian Spirituality for the Twenty-First Century*, London: Hodder & Stoughton.

Sanford, J. A. (1982) *Ministry Burnout*, London: Arthur James Limited.

Sheldrake, P. (1998), *Spirituality and Theology*, London, Darton, Longman and Todd.

Swinton, J. and Mowat, H. (2006), *Practical Theology and Qualitative Research*, London: SCM Press.

Thompson, J., with Pattison, S. and Thompson, R. (2008), *SCM Studyguide to Theological Reflection*, London: SCM Press.

Vanstone, W. H. (1977), *Love's Endeavour, Love's Expense: the Response of Being to the Love of God*, London: Darton, Longman and Todd.

Vanstone, W. H. (1982), *The Stature of Waiting*, London: Darton, Longman and Todd.

Veling, T. A. (2005), *Practical Theology: 'On Earth as it is in Heaven'*, Maryknoll, NY: Orbis Books.

Waller, R. and Ward, B. (eds.) (1999), *An Introduction to Christian Spirituality*, London, SPCK.

Wenham, G. (2003), *Exploring the Old Testament*; Volume 1; The Pentateuch, London: SPCK.

Willimon, W. H. (1988), *Interpretation: A Bible Commentary for Teaching and Preaching*, Atlanta, GA: John Knox Press.

Witcombe, J. (ed.) (2005), *The Curate's Guide: from Calling to First Parish*, London: Church House Publishing.